M
A
S
T
E
R
I
N
G

&

U
S
I
N
G

The Internet for Office Professionals Using Netscape Communicator™ Software

Selected Titles from Napier and Judd

Mastering & Using Microsoft Office 97, Professional Edition

Mastering & Using Microsoft Word 97

Mastering & Using Microsoft Excel 97

Mastering & Using Microsoft PowerPoint 97

Mastering & Using Microsoft Access 97

Mastering & Using the Internet for Office Professionals: Netscape Communicator Edition

Mastering & Using the Internet for Office Professionals: Internet Explorer 4 Edition

Mastering & Using Microsoft Office for Windows 95, Professional Edition

Mastering & Using Microsoft Word 7 for Windows 95

Mastering & Using Microsoft Excel 7 for Windows 95

Mastering & Using the Microsoft Office, Professional Edition (Windows 3.1)

Mastering & Using Microsoft Word 6.0 for Windows 3.1

Mastering & Using Microsoft Excel 5.0 for Windows 3.1

Mastering & Using Microsoft Word for Windows 2.0

Mastering & Using WordPerfect 8

Mastering & Using WordPerfect 7

Mastering & Using WordPerfect 6.1 for Windows

Mastering & Using WordPerfect 6.0a for Windows

Mastering & Using WordPerfect 5.2 for Windows

Mastering & Using WordPerfect 6.0

Mastering & Using WordPerfect 5.1

Mastering & Using Lotus 1-2-3, Release 5.0 for Windows

Mastering & Using Lotus 1-2-3, Release 4.0 for Windows

Mastering & Using Lotus 1-2-3, Release 3.4

Mastering & Using Lotus 1-2-3, Release 3.1/3.1+

Mastering & Using Lotus 1-2-3, Release 3.0

MASTERING & USING

The Internet for Office Professionals Using Netscape Communicator™ Software

H. ALBERT NAPIER & PHILIP J. JUDD

COURSE
TECHNOLOGY

ONE MAIN STREET, CAMBRIDGE, MA 02142

an International Thomson Publishing company I(T)P®

Cambridge • Albany • Bonn • Boston • Cincinnati • London • Madrid • Melbourne • Mexico City
New York • Paris • San Francisco • Singapore • Tokyo • Toronto • Washington

Mastering & Using the Internet for Office Professionals Using Netscape Communicator Software is published by Course Technology.

Acquisitions Editor:	Mark Reimold
Developmental Editor:	Ann Shaffer
Production Editor:	Nancy Benjamin
Composition House:	GEX, Inc.
Text Designer:	Joseph Lee
Illustrator:	Michael Kline
Online Companion Programmer:	Chris Greacen
Offline Companion Programmers:	GEX, Inc., Richard Leinecker

© 1998 by Course Technology
A Division of International Thomson Publishing, Inc.—I(T)P®

For more information contact:

Course Technology
One Main Street
Cambridge, MA 02142

ITP Europe
Berkshire House 168-173
High Holborn
London WCIV 7AA
England

Nelson ITP, Australia
102 Dodds Street
South Melbourne, 3205
Victoria, Australia

ITP Nelson Canada
1120 Birchmount Road
Scarborough, Ontario
Canada MIK 5G4

International Thomson Editores
Seneca, 53
Colonia Polanco
11560 Mexico D.F. Mexico

ITP GmbH
Königswinterer Strasse 418
53277 Bonn
Germany

ITP Asia
60 Albert Street, #15-01
Albert Complex
Singapore 189969

ITP Japan
Hirakawacho Kyowa Building, 3F
2-2-1 Hirakawacho
Chiyoda-ku, Tokyo 102
Japan

ISBN 0-7600-5779-6

Printed in the United States of America

1 2 3 4 5 6 7 8 9 10 01 00 99 98 97

Napier & Judd

I n their over 48 years of combined experience, Al Napier and Phil Judd have developed a tested, realistic approach to mastering and using application software. As both academics and corporate trainers, Al and Phil have the unique ability to help students by teaching them the skills necessary to compete in today's complex business world.

H. Albert Napier, Ph.D. is the Director of the Center on the Management of Information Technology and an Associate Professor in the Jones Graduate School of Administration at Rice University. In addition, Al is a principal of Napier & Judd, Inc., a consulting company and corporate trainer in Houston, Texas, that has trained more than 80,000 people in computer applications.

Philip J. Judd is a former instructor in the Management Department and the Director of the Research and Instructional Computing Service at the University of Houston. Phil now dedicates himself to corporate training and consulting as a principal of Napier & Judd, Inc.

Philip J. Judd   H. Albert Napier, Ph.D.

Preface

At Course Technology we believe that technology will transform the way that people teach and learn. We are very excited about bringing you, instructors and students, the most practical and affordable technology-related products available.

The Development Process

Our development process is unparalleled in the educational publishing industry. Every product we create goes through an exacting process of design, development, review, and testing.

Reviewers give us direction and insight that shape our manuscripts and bring them up to the latest standards. Every manuscript is quality tested. Students whose backgrounds match the intended audience work through every keystroke, carefully checking for clarity and pointing out errors in logic and sequence. Together with our own technical reviewers, these testers help us ensure that everything that carries our name is as error-free and easy to use as possible.

The Products

We show both how and why technology is critical to solving problems in the classroom and in whatever field you choose to teach or pursue. Our time-tested, step-by-step instructions provide unparalleled clarity. Examples and applications are chosen and crafted to motivate students.

Instructor's Resource Kit

All books in the Mastering & Using series are supplemented with an Instructor's Resource Kit (IRK) CD-ROM that includes an integrated array of teaching and learning tools that offer you and your students a broad range of technology-based instructional options. You can also obtain many of these components by accessing the Faculty Online Companion at **www.course.com**.

Items on the Instructor's Resource Kit CD-ROM Include:

Electronic Instructor's Manual:

Written by the authors and quality assurance tested, the electronic Instructor's Manual includes:

- A suggested syllabus
- Instructor's notes and chapter outlines
- Solutions to all end-of-chapter material
- Transparency Masters of key concepts

Student Files

To use this book students must have the Student Disk. Student files needed to complete exercises in the text should be copied to a disk as indicated to create the Student Disk. They can also be posted to a network or stand-alone workstations.

Solution Files

Solution Files represent the correctly completed files that students are asked to create in the end-of-chapter exercises.

Course Test Manager Engine

Course Test Manager is a powerful testing and assessment package that enables instructors to create and print tests from test banks designed specifically for Course Technology titles. In addition, instructors with access to a networked computer lab (LAN) can administer, grade, and track tests online. Students can also take online practice tests, which generate customized study guides that indicate where in the text students can find more information on each question.

Course Test Manager Test Bank

The Course Test Manager Test Bank to accompany your text comes along with the engine on the CD-ROM. The test bank includes multiple-choice, true/false, short answer, and essay questions, many of which include graphics from the text.

If you do not have access to a CD-ROM drive, these components are also available on disk through Course Technology's customer service department.

Online / Offline Companion

Mastering & Using the Internet for Office Professionals Using Netscape Communicator Software is designed as a hands-on tool to help students learn about the Internet and how to perform business-related tasks online. In order to use this textbook, students must have access to either the Online or the Offline Companion that accompanies this book.

Online Companion

Students with an Internet connection can hook up directly to the Online Companion Web page to work through the exercises and examples in this book. The Online Companion is updated by Course Technology to provide students with the most up-to-date links and information.

Offline Companion

Students without Internet access can work through many of the exercises and examples in this book using the Offline Companion that is contained in the Instructor's Resource Kit (IRK) and is available through your instructor. The Offline Companion simulates the environment of the Internet and World Wide Web but does not require that students have access to the Internet or the WWW. Note: All of the hands-on e-mail activities in Chapter 3 require that students have Internet access.

Because the Internet is a constantly changing environment, some Web pages in the Offline Companion may not be exactly as they appear online. These pages have been captured to provide students with an example of what they can find on the Internet. For actual product and company information, students should visit the company sites online.

Mastering & Using the Internet for Office Professionals Using Netscape Communicator Software

The Internet is a worldwide collection of computer networks that allow people to communicate with each other. Everyday, millions of people use the Internet at home and at work to research information, purchase goods and services, and speak to each other via electronic mail and chat rooms. This book introduces students to the Internet and the World Wide Web (WWW) and also to some of the ways in which the Internet and the WWW can be used within the office workplace.

Distinguishing Features

All of the textbooks in the Mastering & Using series share key pedagogical features:

Quick Start Approach

In their many years of teaching experience, Napier and Judd have found that students are more enthusiastic about learning a software application if they can see immediate results. With this in mind, the authors have designed a unique system of instruction which allows students to be able to perform the basic application functions quickly. To get students up and running quickly on the Internet using Netscape Communicator software, this book begins with an overview of the Internet that provides students with an important context of what the "net" is, introduces the Netscape Communicator applications, and teaches students how to use the most popular Internet tool—electronic mail.

Chapter Openers

To help students understand how what they are learning is applicable in a real world setting, chapters in the Mastering & Using series begin with a photo and an accompanying quote from an office professional explaining how they apply the chapter material in their daily lives.

Step-by-Step Instructions and Screen Illustrations

All examples in this text include step-by-step instructions. Screen illustrations are used extensively to help students learn the features of Netscape Communicator software. The authors have found this approach very useful for both novice and more advanced users.

Quick Tip

Placed in the margins next to the relevant material in the chapter, these boxes of information provide students with shortcuts to perform common business-related functions and increase their productivity.

Caution

Based on their years of experience teaching information technology, the authors have placed notes in the margin next to concepts or steps which often cause students difficulty. Each Caution box anticipates the student's possible confusion, and provides methods for avoiding the problem in the future.

Mouse Tip / Menu Tip

Since many functions can be performed in a number of different ways, the authors provide additional instructions in the margin for students about alternative methods of performing a task other than the one that is explained in the body of the chapter.

End-of-Chapter Summary, Commands Review, and Exercises

Each book in the *Mastering & Using* series places a heavy emphasis on providing students with the opportunity to practice and reinforce the skills they are learning through extensive exercises. Each chapter has an extensive summary, commands review, concepts review, and case problem exercises so that students can learn by doing. For a further explanation of each end-of-chapter element see page xiv in this preface.

Appendices

Mastering & Using the Internet contains four appendices to further help students prepare to be successful in the classroom as well as in the workplace. In Appendix A students learn how to get help for each individual Communicator application. In Appendix B, students learn how to set up and use Netscape Netcaster to have the latest information on a variety of topics delivered to their computers. In Appendix C, students learn how to participate in newsgroups using Netscape Collabra. Appendix D provides useful tips for finding information on the Web.

SCANS

In 1992 the U.S. Departments of Labor and Education formed the Secretary's Commission on Achieving Necessary Skills, or SCANS, to study the kinds of competencies and skills that workers must have to succeed in today's workplace. The results of the study were published in a document entitled What Work Requires of Schools: A SCANS Report for America 2000. The in-chapter and end-of-chapter exercises in this book are designed to meet the criteria outlined in the SCANS report and thus help prepare students to be successful in today's workplace. In particular, two special types of case problems emphasize important workplace skills. The Help problems help students find the information they need in order to use the Netscape Communicator software efficiently. The Communicate Your Ideas problems require students to write a few paragraphs, or give a presentation on topics related to the Internet.

Acknowledgments

We would like to thank and express our appreciation to the many fine individuals who have contributed to the completion of this book. We have been fortunate to have reviewers whose constructive comments have been so helpful.

No book is possible without the motivation and support of an editorial staff. We wish to acknowledge with great appreciation the following people at Course Technology: Joseph Dougherty, President and CEO, Course Technology; Mark Reimold, Acquisitions Editor; Ann Shaffer, Product Manager and Development Editor; Susan Roche, Photographer; Nancy Benjamin, Production Editor; Patty Stephan, Production Manager; Roxanne Alexander, Associate Production Manager; Chris Greacen, Webmaster; and Brian McCooey, Manuscript Quality Assurance Project Leader.

We are very appreciative of the personnel at Napier & Judd, Inc., who helped prepare this book. We acknowledge, with great appreciation, the assistance provided by Ollie Rivers in preparing and checking the many drafts of this book and the Instructor's Manual.

We would also like to thank all of the people and their companies that participated in Voices from Business. The participants and their companies appear in this book solely to express how the skills learned in this book are an essential part of their work environment. By appearing in this book, neither the participants nor their companies are in any way endorsing Netscape or any product or company mentioned in this book.

Myrna D'Addario *Course Technology*

Kija Kim *Harvard Design and Mapping Co., Inc.*

Tom Kutter *Open Market, Inc.*

Joseph Lee *Joseph Lee Design*

Yvonne Malcolm *Northeastern University*

Anne-Marie Scoones *Thomas Nelson Australia*

Alison Steeves *Sunnybrook Health Science Centre*

Ken Wilson *Commonwealth Energy Systems*

Within Every Chapter

Numbered Steps—Clear step-by-step directions explain how to complete the specific task. When students follow the numbered steps, they learn quickly how each procedure is performed and what the results will be.

Mouse Tip—Further instructions help students better understand how to use the mouse to perform application tasks.

Quick Tip—Extra information provides shortcuts on how to perform common business-related functions.

I 66 Chapter 4 | Quick Start for Browsing the Web with Navigator

The current Web page appears in the Print Preview window. The Web page preview looks fine, so you can go ahead and print it. To print the Web page:

| STEP 3 | CLICK | the Print button ⟨Print...⟩ on the Print Preview toolbar |

The Print Preview window closes, and the Print dialog box opens. Note that before you print a Web page, you may want to change some of the Web page setup options like margins, print a document header, print the Web page URL, or change the text color to black. Click the Page Setup command on the File menu to view Web page setup options.

| STEP 4 | VERIFY | that the All option button is selected in the Print range group |

| STEP 5 | VERIFY | that 1 is in the Number of copies: text box |

| STEP 6 | CLICK | OK |

A copy of the Napier & Judd Education Services Web page prints.

4.g Returning to the Default Home Page

It is easy to become disoriented and forget your starting point when you browse the Web by following several links to different Web pages. One way to return to your starting point is to reload the default home page.

IN THIS BOOK

Remember that this text assumes the Netscape home page is the default home page. However, you can easily change your default home page by changing the URL entered in the Home Page Location: text box in the Preferences dialog box. To open this dialog box, use the Preferences command on the Edit menu. Do *not* change your default home page unless your instructor gives you permission.

To reload the default Netscape home page:

| STEP 1 | CLICK | the Home button 🏠 on the Navigation toolbar |

In a few seconds, the Netscape home page appears. Because you have found all the information you need on software training, you can close the Navigator application.

| STEP 2 | CLICK | the Close button ✕ on the Navigator title bar |

MOUSE TIP

You can click the Home button on the Navigation toolbar to load the default home page. If you click the Netscape icon to the right of the Stop button on the Navigation toolbar, the Netscape default home page loads.

QUICK TIP

You can attach a Web page to an e-mail message by clicking the Send Page command on the File menu. The Composition window appears with the title of the Web page in the Subject: text box, the Web page URL entered and selected in the Attachment tab, and the URL typed in the message text area.

Within Every Chapter

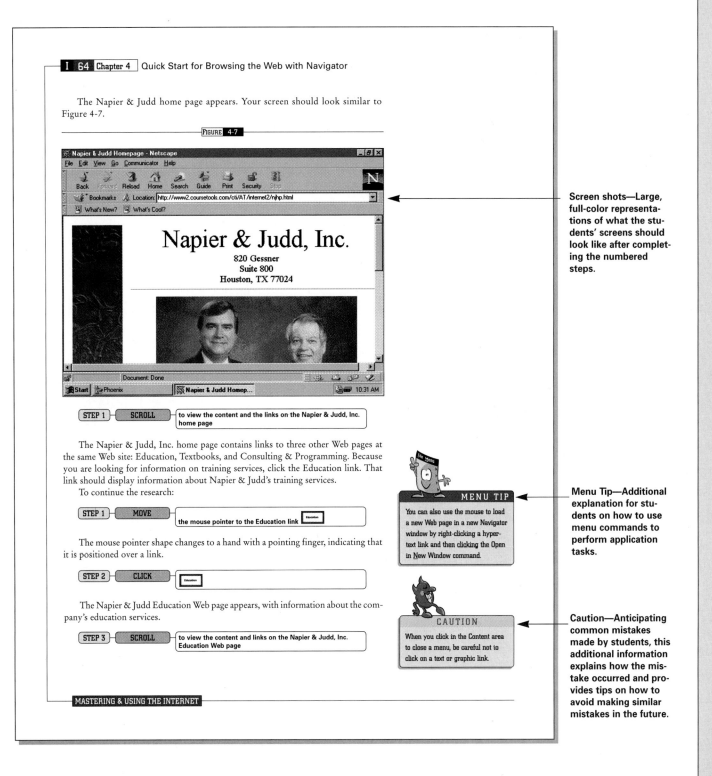

I 64 Chapter 4 | Quick Start for Browsing the Web with Navigator

The Napier & Judd home page appears. Your screen should look similar to Figure 4-7.

FIGURE 4-7

Screen shots—Large, full-color representations of what the students' screens should look like after completing the numbered steps.

STEP 1 — SCROLL | to view the content and the links on the Napier & Judd, Inc. home page

The Napier & Judd, Inc. home page contains links to three other Web pages at the same Web site: Education, Textbooks, and Consulting & Programming. Because you are looking for information on training services, click the Education link. That link should display information about Napier & Judd's training services.

To continue the research:

STEP 1 — MOVE | the mouse pointer to the Education link

The mouse pointer shape changes to a hand with a pointing finger, indicating that it is positioned over a link.

STEP 2 — CLICK |

The Napier & Judd Education Web page appears, with information about the company's education services.

STEP 3 — SCROLL | to view the content and links on the Napier & Judd, Inc. Education Web page

MENU TIP
You can also use the mouse to load a new Web page in a new Navigator window by right-clicking a hypertext link and then clicking the Open in New Window command.

Menu Tip—Additional explanation for students on how to use menu commands to perform application tasks.

CAUTION
When you click in the Content area to close a menu, be careful not to click on a text or graphic link.

Caution—Anticipating common mistakes made by students, this additional information explains how the mistake occurred and provides tips on how to avoid making similar mistakes in the future.

MASTERING & USING THE INTERNET

Online / Offline Companion

Many of the in-chapter and end-of-chapter exercises in this book are designed to be completed using either the Online or the Offline Student Companion.

Students can practice downloading files from the Course Technology Student site.

Text search engine simulates using an Internet search engine.

Students can visit the Course Technology Web site.

Student feedback is welcome at Course Technology.

Hyperlinks allow students to connect to search results quickly.

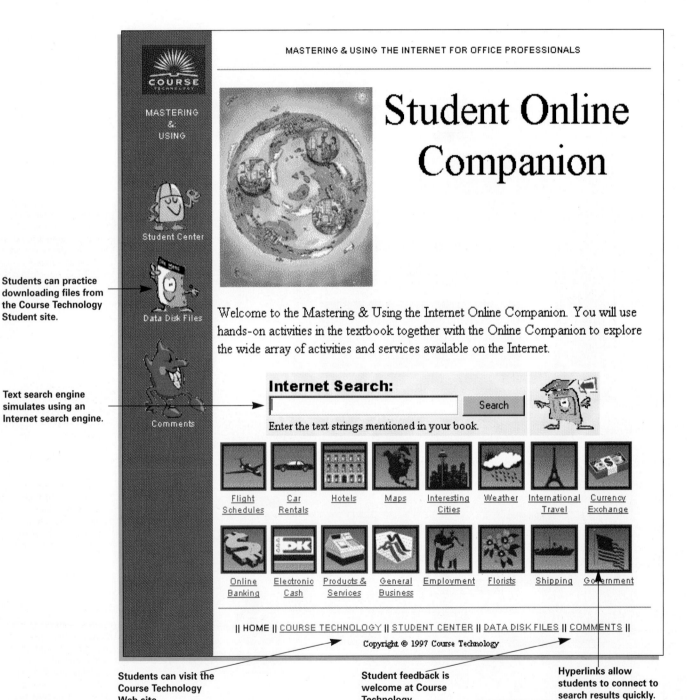

Search Results

Students learn how to search the World Wide Web by using the Web browser simulator. All of the search result pages contained in the Online and Offline Student Companions are linked directly to exercises within this book.

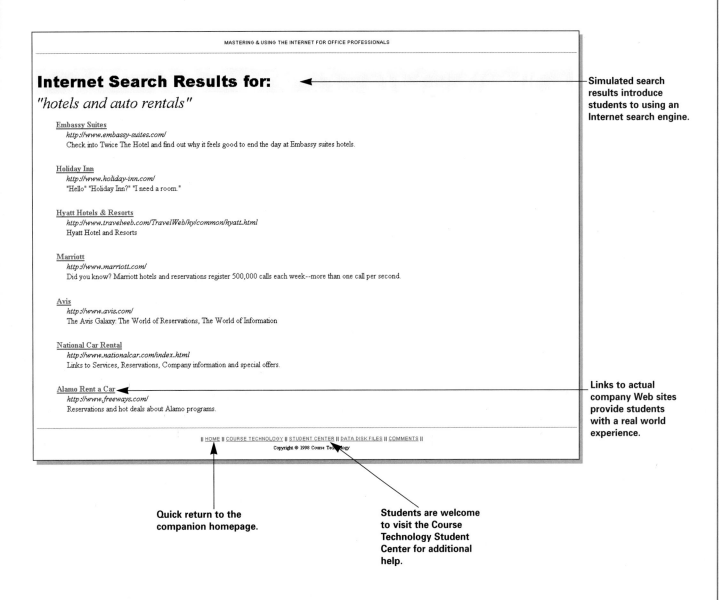

Internet Search Results for:

"hotels and auto rentals"

Simulated search results introduce students to using an Internet search engine.

<u>Embassy Suites</u>
http://www.embassy-suites.com/
Check into Twice The Hotel and find out why it feels good to end the day at Embassy suites hotels.

<u>Holiday Inn</u>
http://www.holiday-inn.com/
"Hello" "Holiday Inn?" "I need a room."

<u>Hyatt Hotels & Resorts</u>
http://www.travelweb.com/TravelWeb/hy/common/hyatt.html
Hyatt Hotel and Resorts

<u>Marriott</u>
http://www.marriott.com/
Did you know? Marriott hotels and reservations register 500,000 calls each week--more than one call per second.

<u>Avis</u>
http://www.avis.com/
The Avis Galaxy: The World of Reservations, The World of Information

<u>National Car Rental</u>
http://www.nationalcar.com/index.html
Links to Services, Reservations, Company information and special offers.

<u>Alamo Rent a Car</u>
http://www.freeways.com/
Reservations and hot deals about Alamo programs.

Links to actual company Web sites provide students with a real world experience.

|| <u>HOME</u> || <u>COURSE TECHNOLOGY</u> || <u>STUDENT CENTER</u> || <u>DATA DISK FILES</u> || <u>COMMENTS</u> ||
Copyright © 1998 Course Technology

Quick return to the companion homepage.

Students are welcome to visit the Course Technology Student Center for additional help.

End-of-Chapter Material

In order to help students reinforce the skills they have learned, each chapter has an extensive summary, commands review, concepts review, skills review, and case problems.

Summary & Commands Review

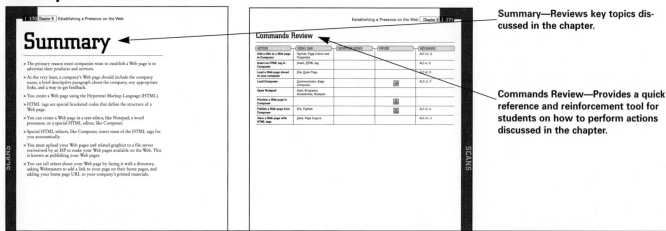

Summary—Reviews key topics discussed in the chapter.

Commands Review—Provides a quick reference and reinforcement tool for students on how to perform actions discussed in the chapter.

Concepts Review

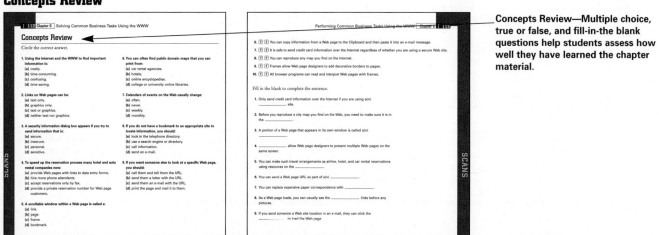

Concepts Review—Multiple choice, true or false, and fill-in-the blank questions help students assess how well they have learned the chapter material.

Case Problems

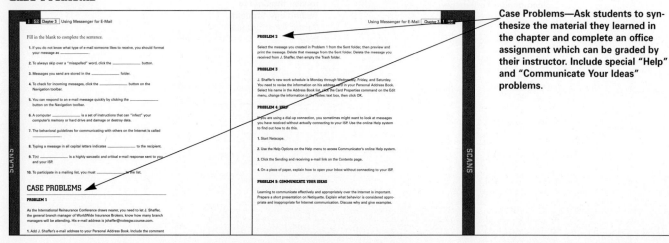

Case Problems—Ask students to synthesize the material they learned in the chapter and complete an office assignment which can be graded by their instructor. Include special "Help" and "Communicate Your Ideas" problems.

Contents

Communicator

Introduction to the Internet

"My job as an administrative assistant demands that I am well-organized and able to perform multiple tasks efficiently. Using the Internet helps me to be more productive. I am able to track packages and receive support from vendors. I am also able to keep our staff informed by e-mail of any important information."

Yvonne Malcolm
administrative assistant

Department of Psychology
Northeastern University
Boston, MA

Chapter Overview:

Today, millions of people use the Internet to shop for goods and services, listen to music, view artwork, conduct research, get stock quotes, keep up-to-date with current events, and send electronic mail. More and more people are using the Internet at work and at home to view and download multimedia computer files containing graphics, sound, video, and text. But what exactly is the Internet? What are its origins? You will learn the answer to these questions in this chapter. You'll also learn how to get connected to the Internet and about some challenges involved in using it.

SNAPSHOT

In this chapter you will learn to:

> Describe the Internet

> Discuss the history of the Internet

> List the services available on the Internet

> Connect to the Internet

> Recognize the challenges of using the Internet

1.a What Is the Internet?

To understand what the Internet is, you first need to be familiar with the concept of a network. A **network** is a group of two or more computers linked by cables, telephone lines, or other communication media (such as satellite signals). The linked computers include a special computer called a **network server**, which stores files and programs that can be used by everyone on the network. Networks are useful because they allow many people to share the software resources stored on the network server as well as hardware resources, such as a printer. See Figure 1-1.

FIGURE 1-1

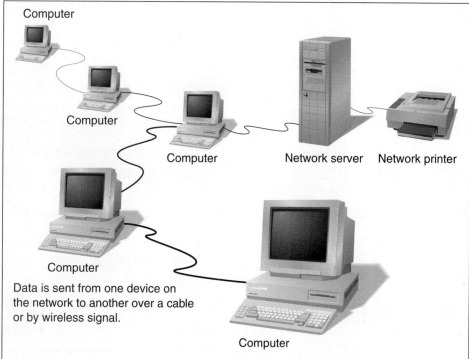

Computer

Computer

Computer

Network server   Network printer

Computer

Data is sent from one device on the network to another over a cable or by wireless signal.

Computer

The **Internet** is a collection of computer networks that allows users to view and transfer information between computers all over the world. The Internet is not a single organization but rather a cooperative effort by multiple organizations managing a variety of different kinds of computers. See Figure 1-2.

FIGURE 1-2

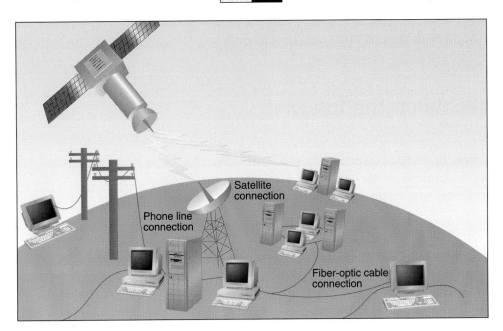

Because the Internet is made up of computers around the world, an Internet user in Texas can retrieve (or **download**) files from a computer in Australia quickly and easily. In the same way, an Internet user in Canada can send (or **upload**) files to another Internet user in France.

IN THIS BOOK

There are many ways to access Internet resources; however, for the activities in this book you will use Netscape Communicator Internet Suite, which includes the Navigator Web browser. This book also assumes you are familiar with Windows 95.

1.b A Brief History of the Internet

The Internet has its origins in the late 1960s, when the U.S. Department of Defense developed a network of military computers called the ARPAnet. Quickly realizing the usefulness of such a network, researchers at colleges and universities began using ARPAnet to share data. In the 1980s, the military portion of the early Internet became a separate network called the MILNET. Meanwhile, the National Science Foundation began overseeing the remaining nonmilitary portions, which it called the NSFnet. Soon, thousands of other government, academic, and business computer networks began connecting to the NSFnet.

By the late 1980s, the term "Internet" was used widely to describe this huge world-wide "network of networks." Recently, a subset of the Internet, called the World Wide Web, has become extremely popular in business, academic, and home environments. As you will learn in Chapter 4, the **World Wide Web (WWW)** presents information in a multimedia format that includes text, graphics, audio, and video.

1.c Services Available on the Internet

The World Wide Web is only one of many services available on the Internet. Table 1-1 describes some of the options. In later chapters, you will learn about sending electronic mail (e-mail), using the World Wide Web, and using search engines. For more detailed information on the remaining topics, see Netscape Communicator's online Help.

TABLE 1-1

CATEGORY	SERVICE	DESCRIPTION
COMMUNICATION	E-mail	Electronic messages sent or received from one computer to another; "e-mail" is short for "electronic mail"
	Newsgroups	Electronic "bulletin boards" where people with common interests (like hobbies or professional associations) post messages (called "articles") that can be read and responded to by other participants around the world; sometimes called Internet discussion groups
	Mailing lists	A service similar to newsgroups except that participants exchange information via e-mail
	Chat groups	Real-time online conversations in which participants type messages to other chat group participants and receive responses they can read on their screens within a few seconds
FILE ACCESS	FTP	A method for sending (uploading) or receiving (downloading) computer files via the File Transfer Protocol (FTP) communication rules
	Gopher	Old method of displaying and downloading files from lists of files located on the Internet at computers called Gopher sites
TERMINAL EMULATION		A method for connecting directly to another computer on the Internet using the TELNET communication rules
SEARCHING TOOLS	Directories	Web tools that help you search for information on the WWW by category
	Search engines	Web tools to help you find specific information on the WWW by searching for specific words or phrases
WORLD WIDE WEB (WWW)	Web sites	Computers where files (or Web pages) containing text, graphics, video, audio, and links to other pages are stored; accessed by using programs called Web browsers

1.d Connecting to the Internet

To connect to the Internet, you need some physical communication medium connected to your computer like network cable or a modem. You also need a communication program that allows your computer to communicate with computers on the Internet. To connect to the World Wide Web, you need a special program called a Web browser (such as Netscape Navigator, included as part of Netscape Communicator), which allows you to move among all the Internet resources quickly and easily. Finally, you need an Internet Service Provider.

INTERNET SERVICE PROVIDERS

After you have set up your computer hardware (the network cable or modem) and installed Netscape Communicator, you must make arrangements to connect to a computer on the Internet. The computer you connect to is called a **host**. Usually, you connect to a host computer via a commercial Internet Service Provider, who sells access to the Internet. An **Internet Service Provider (ISP)** maintains the host computer, provides a gateway, or entrance, to the Internet, and provides electronic "mail boxes" with facilities for sending and receiving e-mail. See Figure 1-3.

FIGURE 1-3

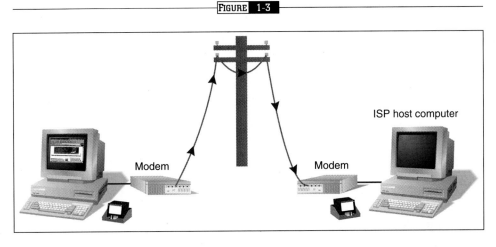

Commercial ISPs usually charge a flat monthly fee for unlimited access to the Internet and e-mail services. Many commercial ISPs supply the communication program and browser program you need to access the Internet. When using a commercial ISP, you usually have to connect to, or log on to, the ISP each time you want to use the Internet. The actual process of logging on varies from one ISP to another. See Figure 1-4.

FIGURE 1-4

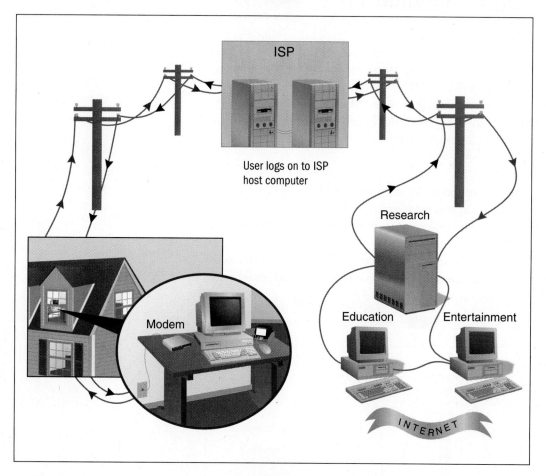

Many large commercial enterprises, colleges, universities, public libraries, and government institutions have networks that are part of the Internet. Their users connect to the Internet through those existing network ISPs rather than through commercial ISPs. Computers connected to such a network often maintain a constant connection to the Internet, which means users never have to worry about logging on.

Once you are connected to the Internet (either via a commercial ISP or an institutional network ISP), you can use a program like Netscape Communicator to access its many services. Accessing the Internet's services involves connecting to other host computers. To do that, you need to be familiar with the "addresses" used to identify computers on the Internet.

INTERNET ADDRESSES

Every host computer on the Internet is identified by a unique Internet address, or **IP address,** that consists of a series of numbers. Computers on the Internet use the IP address numbers to communicate with each other, but it is unlikely that you will ever have to use one yourself (except possibly when you are setting up an ISP connection for the first time). More important is the host computer's descriptive address.

The **descriptive address** specifies the individual computer in the levels of organization, or **domain**, on the Internet. For example, a host computer in the math department at the University of Idaho might be identified as:

raven.math.uidaho.edu

Here, "raven" identifies the specific computer, "math" identifies the department, "uidaho" identifies the university, and the suffix "edu" identifies that the address is for an educational institution. You will find that the descriptive host name is much easier to use and remember than the IP address. See Figure 1-5.

FIGURE 1-5

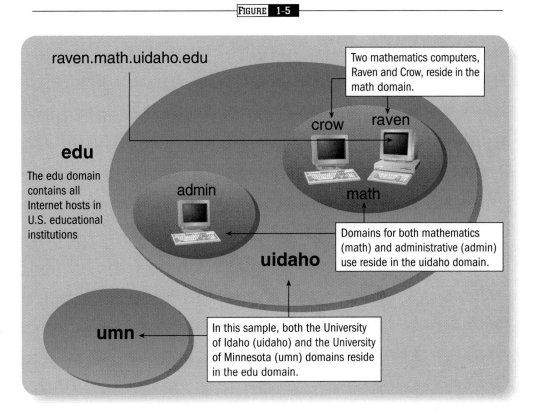

raven.math.uidaho.edu

Two mathematics computers, Raven and Crow, reside in the math domain.

crow   raven

edu

The edu domain contains all Internet hosts in U.S. educational institutions

admin   math

uidaho

Domains for both mathematics (math) and administrative (admin) use reside in the uidaho domain.

umn

In this sample, both the University of Idaho (uidaho) and the University of Minnesota (umn) domains reside in the edu domain.

Table 1-2 identifies the top-level domain (or highest organizational unit on the Internet) names you will see as you work with Internet resources.

TABLE 1-2

TOP-LEVEL DOMAIN	TYPE OF ORGANIZATION
.com	Commercial enterprise
.gov	Government institution
.edu	Educational institution
.mil	Military institution
.net	Computer network
.org	Other organizations

In addition to the domain names shown in Table 1-2, seven new top-level domain names are under consideration: .firm, .store, .web, .arts, .rec, .info, and .nom.

USER NAMES

When you make arrangements to access the Internet via an ISP, you set up a **user name**, which identifies your account with the ISP. Your user name consists of a name you select and the host's descriptive name. User names can be full names, first initial and last names, nicknames, or a group of letters and numbers. For example, the user name for Steve Brown who accesses the Internet via the commercial ISP Xeon Data Systems might be:

```
Steve_Brown@xeon.net
```

where "Steve_Brown" is the user's name, and "xeon.net" is the descriptive name for the ISP's host computer.

RELATED EXTERNAL NETWORKS

There are several commercial networks that are separate from the Internet. In addition to Internet access, these **commercial networks** provide users with a variety of attractively presented features such as online editions of newspapers and magazines, chat groups, access to investment activities, computer games, and special-interest bulletin boards. Popular commercial networks include America Online, CompuServe, Prodigy, and the Microsoft Network. Fees for using a commercial network usually are an hourly rate for a specific number of hours each month (with a per-hour charge for excess time used) or a flat monthly fee for unlimited usage.

USENET is another network that is separate from but closely connected to the Internet. The **USENET network** is a collection of computers that maintain and exchange newsgroup articles and information shared by computer discussion groups.

1.e Challenges of Using the Internet

Using the Internet to send e-mail, read and post articles to newsgroups, chat online, send and receive files, and search for information is fun and exciting. However, there are several challenges involved.

First, because the Internet is used by people all over the world, there is a seemingly endless source of data and information. The sheer size of the Internet sometimes can be intimidating. Using tools such as Uniform Resource Locators (URLs), search engines, and directories to find specific information can help minimize sorting through such a huge volume of information. URLs, search engines, and directories are discussed in more detail in later chapters.

Another potential difficulty is the time it takes for messages and files to travel between computers on the Internet. Communication speeds can be improved by the use of high-speed modems and special telephone lines. Faster Internet communication via cable will be more widely available in the future.

You should also be aware that, because the Internet is a cooperative effort, there are few widely accepted standards. As a result, the presentation of information on the Internet is varied and inconsistent. The Internet is a dynamic environment that changes daily, with new host computers being added and various computer sites no longer being maintained.

There also may be questions about the copyright status of the information you find on the Internet. Remember that the Internet is a largely unregulated environment with few if any controls over what information is published on the WWW or contained in files at FTP sites. It is a good idea to get supporting information from another source before you use any information taken from the Internet to make a critical business decision. Many college and university librarians have Web sites with excellent tips on how to use and evaluate information on the Internet.

Another challenge to using the Internet is the lack of privacy and security for your e-mail and file transmissions. Information sent from one computer to another can travel through many computer systems and networks, where it could be intercepted, copied, or altered. When you access a page on the WWW, it is possible that information such as your e-mail address, which Web pages you view, the type of computer, operating system, and browser you are using, and how you linked to that page can be captured without your knowledge. If you are concerned, take advantage of programs that prevent this type of information from being captured.

Certain browser and server programs on Internet computers can encrypt, or scramble, information during transmission and then decrypt, or unscramble, it at its destination. Commercial activities, such as purchasing an item via credit card or transferring money between bank accounts, can take place in this type of *secure* environment. Be advised, however, that much Internet activity takes place in an *insecure* environment. Government regulations as well as technological methods to ensure privacy and security on the Internet continue to be developed.

CAUTION

Before incorporating an item (such as text or a graphic) you find on the Internet into your own publications, you need to check on the item's copyright status. If it is not copyrighted, or in **public domain**, you can generally use it freely. If the item is copyrighted, you need to seek permission from the copyright holder before using it. If you are unsure about copyright status, *always seek permission.*

During peak day and evening hours, millions of people are connecting to the Internet. During those hours, you may have difficulty connecting to your host computer or to other sites on the Internet.

Summary

> A network is a group of two or more computers linked by cable or telephone lines.

> The Internet is a worldwide "network of networks."

> The Internet began in the late 1960s as the military computer network ARPAnet. By the 1980s, the National Science Foundation assumed responsibility for the nonmilitary portions, and the term "Internet" became widely used.

> The World Wide Web is just one of many services to be found on the Internet.

> Internet users can communicate with each other via e-mail, newsgroups, and online chat groups.

> To access the Internet, your computer must have a physical communication medium, like cable or a modem, and a special communication program.

> An Internet Service Provider (ISP) maintains a host computer on the Internet. To connect to the Internet, you need to connect to the host computer.

> Large commercial enterprises, colleges, and universities often provide Internet access to their employees or students through a special computer network.

> Each host computer has two addresses: an IP address, consisting of a series of numbers, and a descriptive name, based on the computer name and domain of the host.

> Each user has a name that identifies his or her account with an ISP.

> External networks related to the Internet are large commercial networks like America Online, CompuServe, Prodigy, the Microsoft Network, and USENET.

> There are many challenges to using the Internet, including the vast amount of information available, communication speed, the dynamic environment, the lack of presentation standards, and privacy and security issues.

> You should carefully evaluate the validity and copyright status of information you get from the Internet. Confirm any business-critical information from another source. Do not attempt to re-use copyrighted items without permission.

Concepts Review

Circle the correct answer.

1. A network is:
[a] the Internet.
[b] two or more computers linked by cable, telephone lines, or other communication media.
[c] a special computer that is used to store files and programs.
[d] the World Wide Web.

2. To download files from the Internet means to:
[a] retrieve files from a computer connected to the Internet.
[b] send files to a computer connected to the Internet.
[c] search a list of individual files on the Internet.
[d] receive electronic mail messages.

3. The Internet began as a network used for only:
[a] academic research.
[b] business transactions.
[c] government legislation.
[d] military purposes.

4. Which of the following is not a service on the Internet:
[a] ISP.
[b] e-mail.
[c] chat groups.
[d] FTP.

5. In the descriptive name address "poe.english.rice.edu" the word "english" identifies the:
[a] specific computer.
[b] department.
[c] university.
[d] type of organization.
[e] security and privacy.

6. A domain name identifies:
[a] an IP address.
[b] a host computer.
[c] an individual computer within an organization.
[d] an e-mail address.

7. The information you find on the Internet is:
[a] always secure.
[b] sometimes secure.
[c] never secure.
[d] secure when it is encrypted.

8. Which of the following is a valid user name for an ISP account?
[a] Joe Shaffer.xeon.net.
[b] Joe@Shaffer.xeon@net.
[c] .Joe_Shaffer@xeon@net.
[d] Joe_Shaffer@xeon.net.

Circle T if the statement is true or F if the statement is false.

1. T F The World Wide Web is a commercial, for-profit network.

2. T F All host computers on the Internet are identified by a unique Internet address, or IP address, that consists of a series of numbers.

3. T F A host computer's descriptive address specifies the individual computer within a level of organization on the Internet.

4. T F USENET is an old method of displaying and downloading files from lists of files located on the Internet.

5. T F Search engines allow you to search for Web pages by specific words or phrases.

6. (T) (F) Commercial networks provide users with a variety of attractively presented features, such as online editions of newspapers and magazines, chat groups, access to investment activities, computer games, and special-interest bulletin boards.

7. (T) (F) The Internet is a regulated environment with many controls over what information is published on the WWW or contained in files at FTP sites.

8. (T) (F) One challenge of using the Internet is the lack of privacy and security for your e-mail and file transmissions.

Fill in the blank to complete the sentence.

1. A network includes a special computer called a(n) _____, which is used to store files and programs that can then be used by everyone on the network.

2. The _____, a subset of the Internet, presents information in a multimedia format that includes text, graphics, audio, and video.

3. A(n) _____ maintains the host computer, provides a gateway or entrance to the Internet, and provides an electronic "mail box" with facilities for sending and receiving e-mail.

4. The computer you connect to on the Internet is called a(n) _____ computer.

5. When you make arrangements to access the Internet via an ISP, you will also set up a(n) _____ that identifies your account with the ISP.

6. Government institutions are identified by this top-level domain name: _____.

7. Popular _____ networks include America Online, CompuServe, Prodigy, and the Microsoft Network.

8. Certain browser and server programs on Internet computers can _____, or scramble, information during transmission and then _____, or unscramble, it at its destination.

Case Problems

PROBLEM 1: COMMUNICATE YOUR IDEAS

The Internet has many services available, such as e-mail, newsgroups, FTP, and search engines. Many of these services are very useful to businesses. Select a company (real or fictional) and then choose six Internet services. Prepare a presentation that explains at least one way that each service could benefit that company.

PROBLEM 2: COMMUNICATE YOUR IDEAS

Your friend has just purchased an IBM-compatible personal computer for use at home. She asks you to help her set up the computer and then connect it to the Internet. In one or two paragraphs explain how you would connect her computer to the Internet from her home.

SCANS

Using Netscape Communicator Applications

> *At Com Energy, we are able to access data on the Internet and integrate that information into a spreadsheet for our monthly reports. We are also able to share information with our customers through our Web page.*

Ken Wilson
account assistant

*Commonwealth Energy System
Cambridge, MA*

Commonwealth Energy System is an exempt public utility holding company with investments in four operating public utility companies in Massachusetts.

Chapter Overview:

Netscape Communicator is a group, or suite, of applications that allows you to take full advantage of the many services found on the Internet. The standard edition of Netscape Communicator includes the following applications: Netscape Navigator, Netscape Messenger, Netscape Collabra, Netscape Composer, Netscape Netcaster, and Netscape Conference. These applications allow you to browse the World Wide Web, send e-mail, participate in Internet discussion groups, "chat" with other users online, and have information automatically delivered to your desktop from the World Wide Web. You will learn how to perform these tasks in later chapters. For now, you will learn how to start and close some of Netscape Communicator's applications. You will also learn the purpose of each application.

SNAPSHOT

In this chapter you will learn to:

> **Start Netscape Navigator**

> **Start and close Netscape Messenger**

> **Start and close Netscape Collabra**

> **Start and close Netscape Composer**

> **Describe Netscape Conference**

> **Describe Netscape Netcaster**

> **Close Netscape Navigator**

IN THIS CHAPTER

The activities in this chapter assume you are connected to your Internet Service Provider, or ISP. You can start Netscape Communicator applications without being connected to your ISP; however, you may have to clear error messages by clicking the OK button in the error message dialog box as the individual applications try to connect to the WWW or an e-mail account. Your instructor can provide additional instructions if you need to complete the activities in this chapter without connecting to your ISP.

2.a Starting Netscape Navigator

You can start any of the Netscape Communicator applications from the Start menu on the taskbar. In most cases, though, you probably will want to begin with the most frequently used application, Netscape Navigator. You then can start other applications from the Navigator window. Navigator is Netscape's Web **browser**; it allows you to connect to, view, and interact with Web sites all over the world. (You will learn more about Web sites and the World Wide Web in Chapter 4.) To start the Netscape Navigator Web browser from the Start menu:

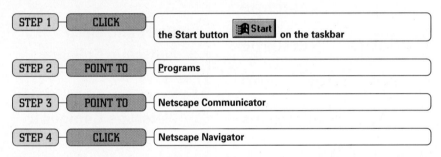

STEP 1 — CLICK — the Start button on the taskbar

STEP 2 — POINT TO — Programs

STEP 3 — POINT TO — Netscape Communicator

STEP 4 — CLICK — Netscape Navigator

CAUTION

If you are using more than one Web browser, a dialog box may appear asking whether Netscape Navigator is your default browser. Follow the steps provided by your instructor regarding your default browser.

The Welcome to Netscape - Netscape window opens. Your screen will probably look like Figure 2-1. Depending on how your version of Navigator is set up, you may see something other than the Welcome to Netscape - Netscape window.

FIGURE 2-1

1. Floating Component Bar

IN THIS BOOK

The World Wide Web is an ever changing environment in which pages are added and modified constantly. For that reason, the Web page illustrations in this book may not be identical to the pages you see on your screen.

The Welcome to Netscape window is actually a Web page. As you will learn in Chapter 4, **Web pages** display information in a multimedia format that can include text, graphics, audio, and video. You will learn how to use Navigator to move among the Web pages on the World Wide Web (a process known as **browsing the Web**) in Chapter 5. For now, you will focus on starting other applications from the Navigator window.

The easiest way to start other applications is to use the buttons on the Component Bar, shown in Figure 2-1. The **Component Bar** is a small toolbar that gives you quick access to most of Netscape Communicator's components. It may appear in a floating window on top of the Navigator window, or it may be **docked** (locked into position) in the bottom-right corner of the Navigator window. If the Component Bar on your screen is not docked, dock it now. To dock the floating Component Bar:

STEP 1 — CLICK — the Close button [X] on the Component Bar title bar

The Component Bar now appears in the bottom-right corner of the Navigator window, as in Figure 2-2.

FIGURE 2-2

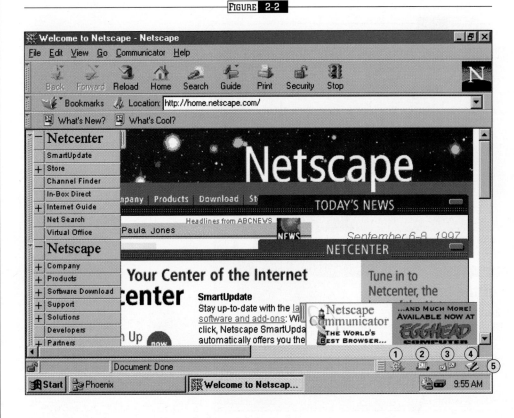

1. Navigator
2. Mailbox
3. Discussion Groups
4. Composer
5. Docked Component Bar

The names of the Component Bar buttons are shown in Figure 2-2.

2.b Starting and Closing Netscape Messenger

You can communicate with others around the world quickly and cheaply 24 hours a day using e-mail. That's why sending e-mail is one of the most popular activities on the Internet. To send, receive, and manage e-mail messages, you use Netscape Communicator's Messenger application. You can start Netscape Messenger by opening the Inbox window. The Inbox is where your incoming e-mail messages are stored. To open the Inbox window and start Netscape Messenger:

STEP 1 — CLICK — the Mailbox button on the Component Bar

STEP 2 — CLICK — the Maximize button , if necessary

QUICK TIP

To float a docked Component Bar, place the mouse pointer on the horizontal lines at the left edge of the Component Bar and drag it to the desired position.

MENU TIP

You also can start the individual Netscape Communicator application windows by using the commands on the Communicator menu.

The Inbox - Netscape Folder window opens. Your screen should look similar to Figure 2-3. If you have messages listed in the Inbox, ignore them for now. You will learn how to read e-mail messages in Chapter 3.

FIGURE 2-3

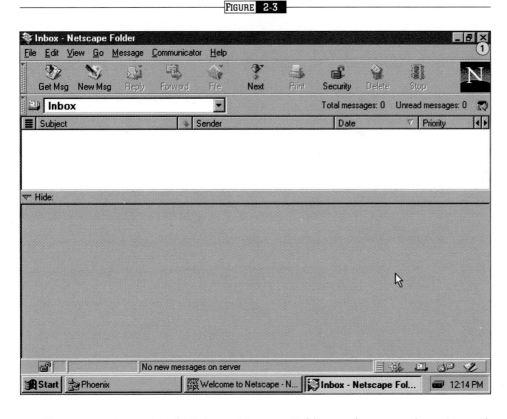

1. Close button

CAUTION

To maintain e-mail security, a password may be required to open the Inbox window. Your instructor will tell you how to enter a password in the Password Entry dialog box, if necessary.

You can use features in the Inbox - Netscape Folder window to send, receive, and manage e-mail messages. You will learn more about the Inbox window in Chapter 3.

Notice that the Component Bar remains in the bottom-right corner of the Messenger window when you start a new application. You can close the Inbox - Netscape Folder window (and most other Communicator applications) by clicking the Close command on the File menu, clicking the Close button on the window's title bar, or right-clicking the application button on the taskbar and then clicking the Close command. The easiest method is to click the window's Close button. To close the Inbox - Netscape Folder window:

STEP 1 | CLICK | the Close button on the title bar

You return to the Navigator window.

2.c Starting and Closing Netscape Collabra

In Internet newsgroups, people discuss a variety of special-interest topics like employment opportunities, the stock market, sports, and business issues. Rather than actually talking to each other, newsgroup participants communicate by posting messages, called

articles, on the global USENET network, which is sometimes referred to as an electronic bulletin board. Interested Internet users around the world can read and respond to articles by writing and posting their own articles, sending e-mail messages to the articles' authors, or both.

Netscape Collabra makes it easy to read and post articles to a newsgroup. You can start Collabra by opening the Message Center window. The Message Center is where your incoming newsgroup messages are stored. To open the Message Center and start Collabra:

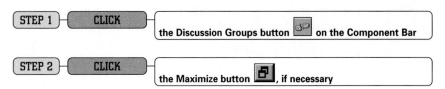

STEP 1 — CLICK — the Discussion Groups button on the Component Bar

STEP 2 — CLICK — the Maximize button, if necessary

The Netscape Message Center window, the primary Collabra window, opens. Your screen should look similar to Figure 2-4. The news server you see highlighted on your screen is the ISP computer that manages your newsgroup services. Your screen probably will be different from the one shown in Figure 2-4. You use the e-mail folders to store incoming and outgoing articles, drafts of articles, and so on.

FIGURE 2-4

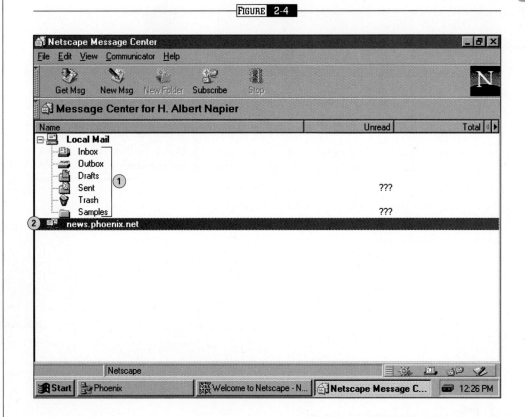

1. E-mail folders
2. News server folder

By posting your own articles and reading those of others, you can take part in Internet discussions on an almost infinite variety of topics. To see a list of the newsgroups provided by your ISP:

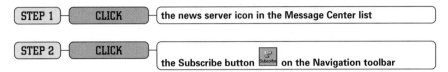

The Communicator: Subscribe to Discussion Groups dialog box opens, and in a moment a list of the available newsgroups appears in the All Groups tab. Your instructor can provide more information on how to subscribe to and participate in newsgroups using the features in this dialog box. For now, you will close the dialog box and then close Collabra. To close the Communicator: Subscribe to Discussion Groups dialog box:

You will close the Netscape Message Center window in the same way you closed the Inbox – Netscape Folder window, by clicking the Close button on the window's title bar.

Again, you return to the Navigator window. From there, you can start yet another Netscape application.

2.d Starting and Closing Netscape Composer

Millions of Internet users download and view Web pages each day using a Web browser like Navigator. Web pages, such as the Welcome to Netscape Web page you see in the Navigator window, provide information about products and services for sale, education, world and local news, weather, sports, finance, and special-interest topics like popular television programs. Schools have Web pages that contain information about enrollment and class schedules. You can create your own Web pages using Netscape Composer. To start Netscape Composer:

The Netscape Composer window opens.

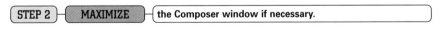

Your screen should look similar to Figure 2-5.

FIGURE 2-5

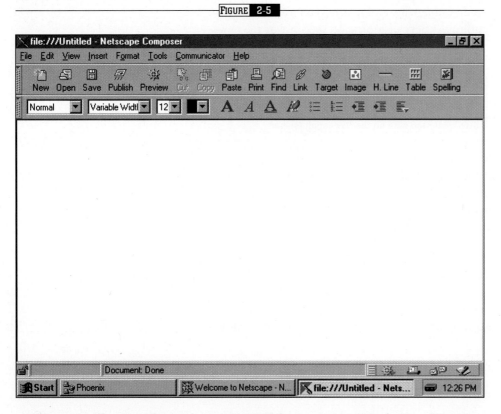

As you will see in Chapter 8, creating a Web page is surprisingly easy. You simply enter and format text (much as you would with a word processor) and then insert pictures and create links to other Web pages. (As you will learn in Chapter 4, **links** are special text or graphics you click to view either a different part of the same Web page or an entirely different Web page.) You can create Web pages in any text editor like Notepad or a word processor like Microsoft Word by entering special codes called HyperText Markup Language (HTML) tags. Web browsers like Navigator use HTML tags to display Web pages. Composer provides shortcuts to use when you are inserting HTML tags. For now, close the Composer window and return to the Navigator window. To close the Composer window:

You return to the Navigator window. The following sections describe the two remaining Netscape applications, Netscape Conference and Netscape Netcaster.

2.e Describing Netscape Conference

Interacting live with others is especially helpful to businesses with offices and employees in different geographical locations. Netscape Conference allows you to communicate live with people all over the world, just as if everyone were gathered in the same room. For example, employees in Boston, London, Toronto, and Sydney could use Composer to participate simultaneously in a live online business conference.

You start Netscape Conference by clicking the <u>C</u>onference command on the Communicator menu. However, before you can use Conference, you must have an appropriate communication hookup through either a network or a modem. (The Setup Wizard walks you through the process of arranging a communication hookup the first time you use Conference.) Then, before you can use any of the Conference features, you must call someone by entering an e-mail address, using a speed-dial number, or a number from the Conference phone books.

2.f Describing Netscape Netcaster

Using the final Netscape application, Netcaster, you can subscribe to "channels," which are Web sites that provide automatic delivery of Web pages of your choice, like local weather reports or news headlines, directly to your computer. The Netcaster application enables you to get the up-to-date information you need without searching the World Wide Web or reading through information that is dated or irrelevant. For example, you may want to have certain stock prices delivered automatically from a Web site to your desktop each day. To start the Netcaster application, you click the <u>N</u>etcaster command on the <u>C</u>ommunicator menu.

QUICK TIP

Netcaster is only available in Communicator version 4.2 and later.

2.g Closing Netscape Navigator

Now that you are familiar with Netscape Communicator's individual applications, you can learn how to use them to take full advantage of the services offered on the Internet. In the next chapter, you will learn more about using Messenger to send and receive e-mail. In Chapters 4–7, you will learn how to use Navigator to perform various business tasks, and in Chapter 8, you will learn how to create a Web page using Composer. To close Navigator:

STEP 1 — CLICK — the Close button ☒ on the Navigator title bar

Summary

> Netscape Communicator consists of six applications: Navigator, for Web browsing; Messenger, for managing e-mail; Collabra, for posting articles to newsgroups; Composer, for creating Web pages; Conference, for managing real-time communication; and Netcaster, for automatic delivery to your desktop of up-to-date information from the World Wide Web.

> The Component Bar contains buttons you can use to start the Messenger, Collabra, and Composer applications.

> You can also start applications with the Communicator command on the menu bar.

> The easiest way to close Communicator applications is to use the Close button on the title bar.

Concepts Review

Circle the correct answer.

1. Netscape Communicator is a:
[a] suite of applications that allow you to use Internet services.
[b] group of applications you use only for e-mail.
[c] Web browser.
[d] word processing application.

2. You use Navigator to:
[a] send and receive e-mail.
[b] read and post articles to a newsgroup.
[c] browse the WWW.
[d] create a Web page.

3. The Component Bar is a:
[a] menu that provides quick access to most of Communicator's applications.
[b] toolbar that provides quick access to most of Communicator's applications.
[c] list of all the newsgroups to which you subscribe.
[d] group of icons for inserting HTML tags.

4. Which Communicator application do you use to send and receive e-mail?
[a] Collabra.
[b] Netcaster.
[c] Navigator.
[d] Messenger.

5. Which method does not close a Communicator application?
[a] Right-click the Component Bar.
[b] Click the application Close button on the title bar.
[c] Right-click the application button on the taskbar, then click Close.
[d] Click the Close command on the File menu.

6. Which Communicator application do you use to read and post newsgroup articles?
[a] Collabra.
[b] Netcaster.
[c] Navigator.
[d] Messenger.

SCANS

7. The Message Center stores:
- [a] e-mail messages.
- [b] viewed Web pages.
- [c] speed-dial numbers.
- [d] incoming newsgroup messages and e-mail folders.

8. Before you can use the Conference application, you must:
- [a] open Messenger.
- [b] have an appropriate communication hookup.
- [c] be on a network.
- [d] close any other open Communicator applications.

9. Special text and graphics you click to display another Web page are called:
- [a] articles.
- [b] browsers.
- [c] links.
- [d] HTML tags.

10. The Netcaster application provides:
- [a] an inbox for e-mail messages.
- [b] delivery of select Web pages directly to your computer.
- [c] tools for creating Web pages.
- [d] a message center for Internet discussion group messages.

Circle [T] if the statement is true or [F] if the statement is false.

1. [T] [F] A Web browser allows you to connect to and interact in newsgroups.

2. [T] [F] You can start any Communicator application from the Start menu.

3. [T] [F] The docked Component Bar appears in its own window at the top of the Navigator window.

4. [T] [F] E-mail is managed with the Messenger application.

5. [T] [F] The Inbox – Netscape Folder window has features you can use to send, receive, and manage e-mail messages.

6. [T] [F] Newsgroup participants communicate over the USENET network.

7. [T] [F] The Message Center window allows you to send and receive e-mail messages.

8. [T] [F] Composer provides shortcuts for creating your own Web pages.

9. [T] [F] You cannot create Web pages in a word processor, such as Microsoft Word.

10. [T] [F] To close Communicator, you click the Close button on the Component Bar.

Fill in the blank to complete the sentence.

1. _____ includes Navigator, Messenger, Collabra, Composer, Netcaster, and Conference.

2. Navigator is Netscape's _____.

3. _____ display information in a multimedia format that can include text, graphics, audio, and video.

4. A toolbar that is locked in position is_____.

5. The Mailbox button on the Component Bar opens the _____ window.

6. Newsgroup participants communicate by posting ＿＿＿＿＿＿ on the global USENET network.

7. Netscape Composer enables you to create your own ＿＿＿＿＿＿.

8. You create Web pages by entering special codes called ＿＿＿＿＿＿.

9. Employees in Boston, London, Toronto, and Melbourne could participate simultaneously in a live online business conference using ＿＿＿＿＿＿.

10. With Netcaster you can subscribe to ＿＿＿＿＿＿ to receive automatic delivery of Web pages of your choice.

Case Problems

PROBLEM 1

Explore starting and closing Communicator applications as follows:

1. Start Navigator from the Programs command on the Start menu.

2. Start Collabra from the Component Bar.

3. Close Collabra from the Control-menu icon.

4. Start Messenger from the Component Bar.

5. Close Messenger from the window button on the taskbar.

6. Start Composer from the Communicator menu.

7. Close Composer from the title bar.

8. Close Navigator from the title bar.

9. Start Messenger from the Programs command on the Start menu.

10. Close Messenger from the File menu.

PROBLEM 2: HELP

Start Navigator. Review the commands available on the Help menu. List the different options available and the types of information they contain. (If you are unfamiliar with using a Help system, see Appendix A.)

PROBLEM 3: COMMUNICATE YOUR IDEAS

Netscape Communicator includes six applications that enable you to fully utilize the Internet services. Select a company (real or fictional) and then write one or two paragraphs that describe how that business might use each application to enhance its productivity.

Using Messenger for E-Mail

" *My sales territory spans many miles and traveling to each customer is difficult. Using FTP and e-mail, I am able to supply information and answer customer questions within a fraction of the time and cost that it would take for me to travel and send conventional mail.* "

Anne-Marie Scoones
higher education representative

College and Professional Division
Thomas Nelson Australia
Suite 4, 727 Stanley Street
Woolloongabba QLD 4102 Australia

Thomas Nelson Australia is a division of ITP involved in publishing educational material for primary, secondary, and college level educators.

Chapter Overview:

In Chapter 2, you learned how to use the Component Bar to open Communicator applications. You also learned several methods to close the applications. In this chapter, you will learn more about using the Messenger application to access one of the primary Internet services, electronic mail. Electronic mail, commonly called e-mail, allows Internet users around the world to communicate easily and quickly. You will learn how to compose, send, receive, reply to, and forward e-mail messages. You also will learn about privacy and security issues and how to use proper Internet etiquette, or "Netiquette." Finally, you will learn how to participate in mailing lists.

SNAPSHOT

In this chapter you will learn to:

> **Identify the importance of using e-mail**

> **Define the components of the Inbox window**

> **Describe e-mail addresses**

> **Use the Address Book**

> **Compose e-mail messages**

> **Send e-mail messages**

> **Receive e-mail messages**

> **Reply to e-mail messages**

> **Print e-mail messages**

> **Delete e-mail messages**

> **Recognize e-mail privacy and security issues**

> **Use Netiquette**

> **Participate in mailing lists**

3.a Identifying the Importance of Using E-Mail

Sending messages electronically is one of the most popular uses of the Internet. Much of that popularity is because you can transmit e-mail messages at any time of the day or night, to a co-worker or a client across town or around the world. What's more, replying to an e-mail message is as easy as clicking a button on a toolbar. That means you can count on getting quick replies to all your e-mail correspondence, rather than waiting days for an important client to return your phone call. Yet another advantage to e-mail messages is that they cost less than sending paper letters or faxes or making long-distance telephone calls. Once you learn the basics of sending and receiving e-mail, you will see that it is often the most efficient and cost-effective way to communicate both business and personal messages.

For example, suppose you are Casey Rivers, the office manager for WorldWide Insurance Brokers, Inc, a large insurance brokerage firm in Boston. Your firm specializes in insurance for large commercial and industrial accounts, and its branch offices in Toronto, Sydney, and London provide commercial insurance services to clients throughout the world. Each day you need to communicate with both clients and international branch office personnel quickly. To save time and money, you prefer to use e-mail. In the following sections, you will send e-mail to several of your firm's branch managers.

IN THIS CHAPTER

Before you begin the activities in this chapter, you should connect to your ISP. If you do not have an ISP connection, you will be unable to complete the hands-on activities in this chapter. It is assumed that you are familiar with entering and selecting text in the Windows 95 environment.

3.b Defining the Components of the Inbox Window

Before you begin, you need to start Navigator.

| STEP 1 | START | Navigator from the desktop icon or from the Start menu |

Messenger has several windows you can use to compose, send, receive, and review e-mail messages. As you learned in Chapter 2, the Inbox window is the primary Messenger window. To open the Inbox window:

| STEP 1 | CLICK | the Mailbox button on the Component Bar |

| STEP 2 | CLICK | The Maximize button 🗗 if necessary |

CAUTION

If you see a Password Entry dialog box, see your instructor for directions.

Your screen should look similar to Figure 3-1.

FIGURE 3-1

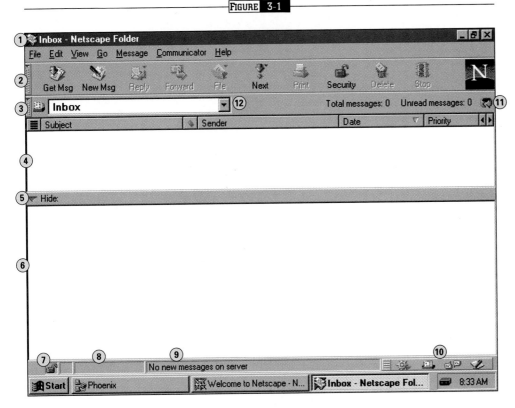

1. Menu bar
2. Navigation toolbar
3. Location toolbar
4. Message List pane
5. Message pane control icon
6. Message pane
7. Security indicator
8. Progress bar
9. Status message area
10. Component Bar
11. Message Center
12. Folder quick-access

The **Menu bar** is located below the title bar and provides access to commands you can use to compose, send, and receive e-mail messages.

The **Navigation toolbar,** located below the Menu bar, provides shortcuts to frequently used menu commands. When you move the mouse pointer to a button on a toolbar, a brief description of the action you perform with the button appears in a yellow text box below the button.

The **Location toolbar** provides quick access to the mail folders where your sent, received, and deleted e-mail messages are stored. This toolbar contains the **Folder quick-access menu,** which in turn contains a drop-down list of mail folders such as the Sent and Trash folders. When you send e-mail, a copy is saved automatically in the **Sent folder,** where it remains until you delete it. New messages are stored in the **Inbox folder.** The Trash folder contains all the e-mail messages you have deleted from the Inbox and Sent folders. Those messages remain in the **Trash folder** until you "empty" it or remove the messages permanently. You can view the contents of a folder by selecting a folder from the list.

Next to the Folder quick-access menu, the Location toolbar shows the total number of messages and the total number of unread messages. Finally, on the far right of the Location toolbar is the **Message Center** button, which you can use to show a list of all the mail folders.

The **Message List pane** is located below the Location toolbar and contains the message header information for incoming messages. As you will see later in this chapter, the message header usually consists of four lines: the subject, date, from, and to information from the incoming e-mail message.

The **Message pane** is located below the Message List pane and contains the body of the message selected in the Message List pane.

The **Message Pane control icon** is located on the divider between the Message List pane and the Message pane. You can use it to hide the Message pane when you want to view a long list of incoming messages in the Message List pane and do not want to view the contents of any individual message. When the Message pane is hidden, the Message Pane control icon appears at the left end of the status bar.

The status bar below the message pane contains the **Security indicator,** which identifies whether the transmission is secure or insecure. (You will learn about some important issues related to the security of Internet transmissions in Chapter 5.) To the right of the Security indicator is the **Progress bar,** which contains information about the progress of downloading e-mail messages from your ISP, the Status message area, and the **Component Bar,** which you learned about in Chapter 2. (If your Component Bar is in a different position from the one in Figure 3.1, see "Starting Netscape Navigator" in Chapter 2 for directions on docking the Component Bar in the bottom-right corner of the screen.)

3.c Describing E-Mail Addresses

Suppose you need to send a message to the branch manager in the Toronto office. Before you can send the message, you must know the branch manager's e-mail address. An e-mail address consists of a name, the "at" symbol (@), and the descriptive host name described in Chapter 1. An e-mail address is usually the same as the User name (also discussed in Chapter 1). For example, the e-mail address for Elizabeth Stone who has Internet access via Xeon Systems might be:

estone@xeon.net

where "estone" is the User name, and "xeon.net" is the descriptive host name.

Many "people-finder" directories can be accessed online, but none provides a comprehensive list of e-mail addresses. Often the best way to get someone's e-mail address simply is to ask. Also, many companies now include e-mail addresses on letterheads and business cards.

The e-mail address for the Toronto branch manager, M. Barrett, is:

mbarrett@notesgw.course.com

Once you know an e-mail address, it is easy to store it for future use in your Personal Address Book. In the next section, you will store the e-mail addresses of World-Wide's branch managers in your Personal Address Book.

3.d Using the Address Book

Because you often send e-mail to M. Barrett, you decide to add the e-mail information to your Personal Address Book, Messenger's electronic address book. Adding address information to the address book is a simple process. For example, if you want to add the e-mail address from a message you already have in your Inbox, you can select the message header in the Message List pane and then click the Add to Address Book command on the Message menu. You also can right-click a selected message header in the Message List pane and then click the Add to Address Book command to automatically add the address. Finally, you can click the Address Book command on the Communicator menu to add a name and e-mail address to your Personal Address Book manually. Because you have not yet received any e-mail messages, you need to enter the branch managers' e-mail addresses in your Personal Address Book manually.

To open the Address Book window from the menu:

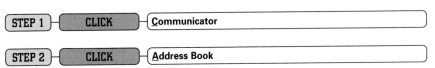

Your screen should look similar to Figure 3-2.

FIGURE 3-2

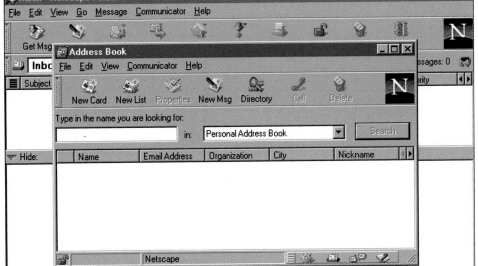

To create a new card for M. Barrett:

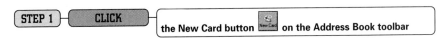

The New Card dialog box opens. Now you can enter a name, organization, title, and e-mail address in the Name tab. You can use the Contact tab to enter a mailing address and phone number, if desired. Your screen should look similar to Figure 3-3.

FIGURE 3-3

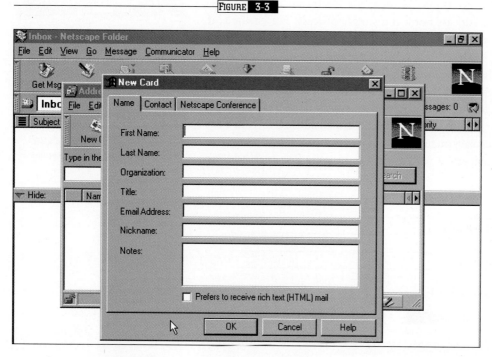

MENU TIP

You can double-click a message header in the Message list pane to add the address to your Address Book.

To add the e-mail address:

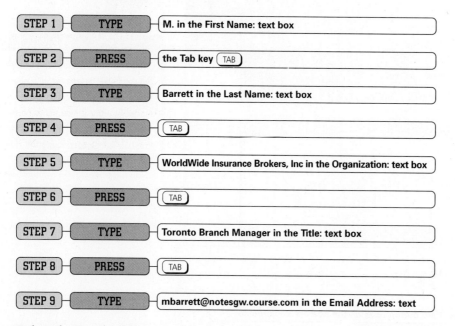

STEP 1	TYPE	M. in the First Name: text box
STEP 2	PRESS	the Tab key (TAB)
STEP 3	TYPE	Barrett in the Last Name: text box
STEP 4	PRESS	(TAB)
STEP 5	TYPE	WorldWide Insurance Brokers, Inc in the Organization: text box
STEP 6	PRESS	(TAB)
STEP 7	TYPE	Toronto Branch Manager in the Title: text box
STEP 8	PRESS	(TAB)
STEP 9	TYPE	mbarrett@notesgw.course.com in the Email Address: text

Below the Email Address: text box is the Nickname: text box, where you can enter an abbreviation or shortcut for the e-mail address. It is not necessary to use a nickname for M. Barrett. The Notes: text box, which you will also leave blank, provides an area in which you can enter additional information, such as the person's work schedule, birthday, or favorite restaurant. The check box at the bottom of the Name tab is a reminder about the type of e-mail the person likes to receive. You can format your e-mail messages as HTML (HyperText Markup Language) text, which can be read in a Web browser, or you can send plain-text messages. If you know the person you are adding to your Personal Address Book can receive HTML messages, indicate that by checking the Prefers to receive rich text (HTML) mail check box. If you are not certain, it is better to send only plain-text messages. To accept the new entry:

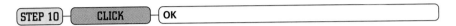

STEP 10 ‐ CLICK ‐ OK

M. Barrett's e-mail address is added to your Personal Address Book. Your screen should look similar to Figure 3-4.

FIGURE 3-4

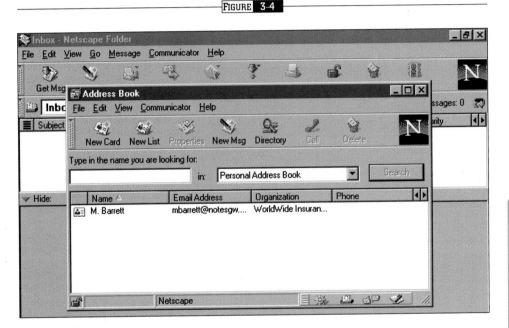

Continue by adding the following two e-mail addresses in Table 3-1:

TABLE 3-1

NAME	ORGANIZATION	TITLE	E-MAIL ADDRESS
B. Witherspoon	WorldWide Insurance Brokers, Inc	Sydney Branch Manager	bwspoon@ notesgw.course.com
C. Jones	WorldWide Insurance Brokers, Inc	London Branch Manager	jonesy@ notesgw.course.com

You are finished adding e-mail addresses to the Address Book. Before you close the Address Book window, note the Search button under the Netscape logo. You can use the Search button to search for e-mail addresses from the Address Book window. To search the available address books and online directories, (1) enter the name you are looking for in the text box below the Address Book toolbar; (2) click the address book/directories list arrow and select the appropriate address book or directory; and (3) click the Search button to the right of the list box.

To close the Address Book window:

STEP 1 ‐ CLICK ‐ the Close button ☒ on the Address Book window title bar

3.e Composing E-Mail Messages

Now you are ready to compose a message to the Toronto branch manager about the upcoming International Reinsurance Conference to be held in Boston on the 2nd of next month. You also want to send a copy of your e-mail to the Sydney and London branch managers.

First, you need to open the Composition window. To open the Composition window:

MENU TIP

You can open the Composition window by clicking the New Message command on the Message menu.

STEP 1 ── CLICK ── the New Msg button on the Navigation toolbar

The Composition window opens. Your screen should look similar to Figure 3-5.

── FIGURE 3-5 ──

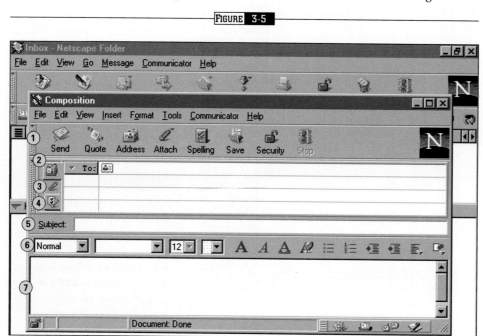

1. Message toolbar
2. Address List tab
3. Attachments List tab
4. Message Options tab
5. Subject area
6. Composer toolbar
7. Composition area

The Composition window is made up of three main parts: the Address List tab, the Subject: text box; and the Composition area. You enter the e-mail addresses of the persons who should receive the message in the Address List tab.

You enter a brief description of the message in the Subject: text box. You enter the message itself in the Composition area. You can use the formatting features on the Composer toolbar located directly above the Composition area to create HTML-formatted messages. Because the branch managers prefer to receive plain-text messages, you will not use those formatting features.

The first step in composing an e-mail message is to enter the recipient's e-mail address. Note that the insertion point appears in the To: address line. You can type an e-mail address on that line, or you can select an e-mail address from your Personal Address Book. To select an address from the Address Book, click the Address button on the Composition toolbar.

QUICK TIP

The Attachments List tab allows you to attach files to your e-mail messages. The Message Options tab contains special e-mail options you can set for the message. For more information on attaching files and setting special message options, see online Help.

To select the e-mail addresses from your Personal Address Book:

STEP 2 — CLICK — the Address button [Address] on the Message toolbar

The Select Addresses dialog box opens. Your screen should look similar to Figure 3-6.

FIGURE 3-6

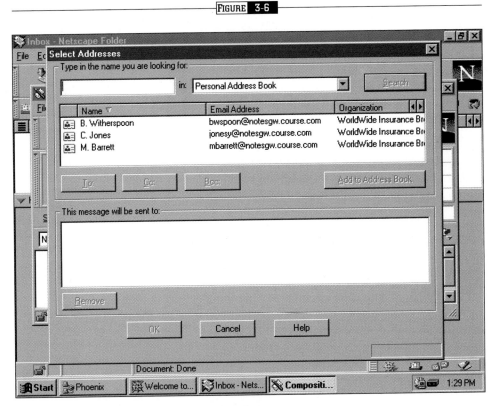

QUICK TIP

You can sort the items in the address list window in ascending or descending order by name, e-mail address, organization, city, or nickname by clicking the column header button above the desired column in the list.

To send a blind copy of a message, select the e-mail address in the Select Addresses dialog box and click the Bcc: button. A blind copy will not show the e-mail address of the person receiving the copy.

STEP 3 — CLICK — M. Barrett in the address list

STEP 4 — CLICK — the To: button

STEP 5 — SELECT — B. Witherspoon and C. Jones by holding down the Shift key while you click each name

STEP 6 — CLICK — the Cc: button

The e-mail addresses are added to the This message will be sent to: list box. To accept the e-mail addresses:

STEP 7 — CLICK — OK

The e-mail address for M. Barrett is added to the To: address line, and the other branch managers' e-mail addresses are added to the Cc: address lines.

To add a subject line to the message:

STEP 1 — PRESS — the Tab key [TAB]

STEP 2 — TYPE — International Reinsurance Conference

Now enter the body of the message. Type the message *exactly* as it is presented in Step 4, below. You will spell check the message later in this section. To enter the body of the message:

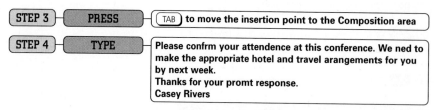

STEP 3 — PRESS — (TAB) to move the insertion point to the Composition area

STEP 4 — TYPE — **Please confrm your attendence at this conference. We ned to make the appropriate hotel and travel arangements for you by next week.**
Thanks for your promt response.
Casey Rivers

Now that you have composed your e-mail message, you are ready to send it. You will do that in the next section.

3.f Sending E-Mail Messages

It is good practice to check the spelling of a message before you send it. You can do that by using either the Check Spelling command on the Tools menu or the Spelling button on the Message toolbar. To check the spelling:

STEP 1 — CLICK — the Spelling button [Spelling] on the Message toolbar

The Check Spelling dialog box opens. Your screen should look similar to Figure 3-7.

FIGURE 3-7

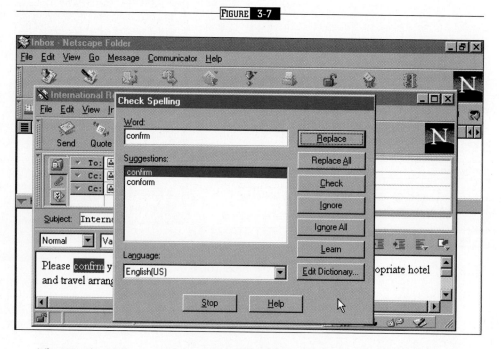

The Word: text box contains the first misspelled word, "confrm." The Suggestions: list box shows possible replacement words. You can type the correct word in the Word: text box or double-click a replacement word in the Suggestions: list box; then click the Replace button to correct the misspelled word. You can also double-click a replacement word to correct the misspelled word. To ignore the misspelled word in a specific instance, click the Ignore button. The Ignore All button allows you to ignore the misspelled word each time it occurs during the current spelling-check session. If you want to stop the spelling-check process, click the Stop button. To close the Check Spelling dialog box after the process is completed, click the Done button when it appears.

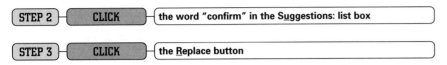

| STEP 2 | CLICK | the word "confirm" in the Suggestions: list box |
| STEP 3 | CLICK | the Replace button |

The next misspelled word, "attendence," appears in the Word: text box. To correct the misspelled word:

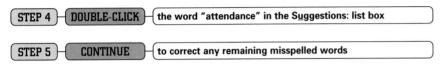

| STEP 4 | DOUBLE-CLICK | the word "attendance" in the Suggestions: list box |
| STEP 5 | CONTINUE | to correct any remaining misspelled words |

To close the Check Spelling dialog box when the process is completed:

| STEP 6 | CLICK | the Done button |

Now you are ready to send the message to all the branch managers.

| STEP 1 | CLICK | the Send button [Send] on the Message toolbar |

The Sending Message dialog box opens, showing the transmission's progress. To stop the transmission before completion, click the Cancel button in the dialog box. After the messages have been transmitted, the Composition dialog box closes.

The message is now stored in a mail folder named "Sent," where it will remain until you decide to delete it. You can review messages stored in the Sent folder by clicking the Folder quick-access menu list arrow on the Location toolbar and then clicking the Sent icon. To review the message to the Toronto branch manager:

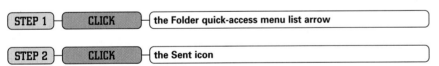

| STEP 1 | CLICK | the Folder quick-access menu list arrow |
| STEP 2 | CLICK | the Sent icon |

The top portion of the Message pane shows information about each message stored in the Sent folder. The information (which usually includes the recipient's name and the subject) is called the **message header**. (You can choose to view more or less message header detail by clicking the All, Normal, or Brief subcommands under the Headers command on the View menu.) To view a message, you first must select its header in the Message pane:

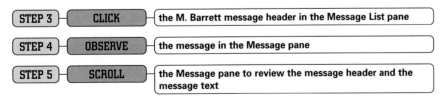

STEP 3	CLICK	the M. Barrett message header in the Message List pane
STEP 4	OBSERVE	the message in the Message pane
STEP 5	SCROLL	the Message pane to review the message header and the message text

After you select the header, the message itself appears below the message header.

After you have reviewed the message you sent to M. Barrett, you need to return to the Inbox window. To open the Inbox window:

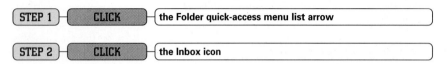

| STEP 1 | CLICK | the Folder quick-access menu list arrow |
| STEP 2 | CLICK | the Inbox icon |

After you compose and send an e-mail message, you usually receive a reply from the person who received the message. Leave the Inbox window open so you can get any incoming messages in the next section.

3.g Receiving E-Mail Messages

Messenger will check your ISP mail server periodically to see if you have any new incoming messages. (With dial-up services, which most people use at home, you probably will need to log on and then check for new messages.) If you are browsing the Web when a new message arrives, a green arrow will appear to the left of the Mailbox icon on the Component Bar. You also can check for incoming messages at any time by clicking the Mailbox icon. If you click the Mailbox icon when there is no incoming mail at the ISP mail server, Messenger will display the information "No new messages on server."

To check for incoming messages stored at your ISP mail server:

| STEP 1 | CLICK | the Get Msg button on the Navigation toolbar |

In a few seconds, a message from M. Barrett is retrieved from your ISP mail server. To view the contents of the message from M. Barrett:

| STEP 2 | CLICK | the M. Barrett message header in the Message List pane |

The message appears in the Message pane.

| STEP 3 | SCROLL | the Message pane window to read the entire message |

3.h Replying to E-Mail Messages

M. Barrett has replied to your e-mail message and is confirming his attendance at the International Reinsurance Conference. He also asks you to make some travel arrangements for him. When you receive an e-mail message, you can reply to it using either menu commands or a toolbar button. The e-mail address of the sender and the message contents will be added to the Composition window automatically.

Because M. Barrett's e-mail address has been designed to provide an automatic response, you will not actually reply to M. Barrett's message. You will only open and review the Composition window and then close it. If you did send a reply, you would receive the same automatic response from M. Barrett, duplicating his original message.

To open the Composition window in reply to M. Barrett's message:

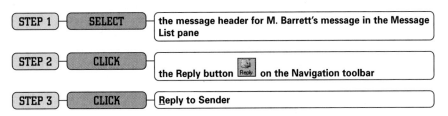

STEP 1	SELECT	the message header for M. Barrett's message in the Message List pane
STEP 2	CLICK	the Reply button on the Navigation toolbar
STEP 3	CLICK	Reply to Sender

The Composition window opens. Notice that the To: text box already contains M. Barrett's e-mail address, and the message area contains the text of M. Barrett's message to you. The insertion point is at the beginning of the message text. To close the Composition window without replying:

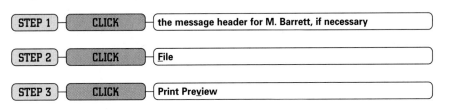

| STEP 4 | CLICK | the Close button on the Composition window title bar |
| STEP 5 | CLICK | Yes to close the confirmation dialog box |

By composing, sending, and replying to e-mail, you have made important arrangements regarding the International Reinsurance Conference in Boston. In the next section, you will learn how to print e-mail messages so you can save a hard copy for your files.

3.i Printing E-Mail Messages

You can easily print a paper copy of an e-mail message. Before you do that, though, it is a good idea to preview your printed message. That way, you can adjust margins and other print settings before you actually print the document.

To preview the message:

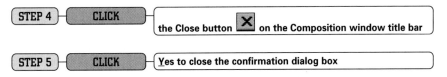

STEP 1	CLICK	the message header for M. Barrett, if necessary
STEP 2	CLICK	File
STEP 3	CLICK	Print Preview

MOUSE TIP

You can reply to a selected message quickly by clicking the Reply button on the Navigation toolbar.

QUICK TIP

You can forward an e-mail message to another e-mail address by clicking the Forward or Forward Quoted command on the Message menu, by right-clicking a message header and clicking Forward or Forward Quoted, or by clicking the Forward button on the Navigation toolbar.

MENU TIP

To preview a message before you print it, click the Print Preview command on the File menu. You can print selected message(s) by clicking the Print command on the File menu. You also can print a message by right-clicking the message header and clicking Print Message.

The message appears in the Print Preview window. Your screen should look similar to Figure 3-8.

FIGURE 3-8

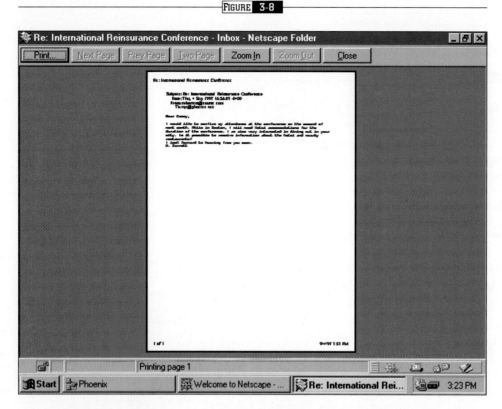

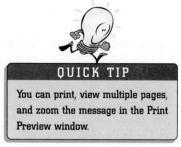

QUICK TIP

You can print, view multiple pages, and zoom the message in the Print Preview window.

The message's layout looks fine, so you do not need to adjust any settings. You will print the message from the Print Preview window. To print the message:

STEP 1 — CLICK

The Print button [Print...] on the Print Preview toolbar

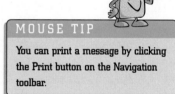

MOUSE TIP

You can print a message by clicking the Print button on the Navigation toolbar.

The Print dialog box opens. Your screen should look similar to Figure 3-9.

FIGURE 3-9

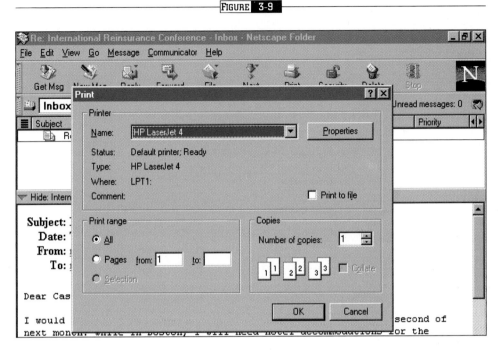

Use the Print dialog box to select specific pages, the number of copies, and the printer properties. To print one copy of all the pages:

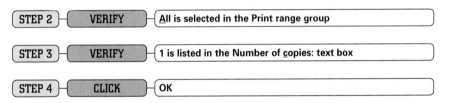

STEP 2 — VERIFY — **All is selected in the Print range group**

STEP 3 — VERIFY — **1 is listed in the Number of copies: text box**

STEP 4 — CLICK — **OK**

One copy of the original message to M. Barrett is printed. Next, you will learn how to delete e-mail messages you no longer need.

3.j Deleting E-Mail Messages

To delete e-mail messages stored in the Inbox and Sent folders, you move them to the Trash folder and then empty the Trash folder. Suppose, for example, that you want to delete the reply message from M. Barrett that is still stored in the Inbox folder.

To delete the Auto Response from M. Barrett:

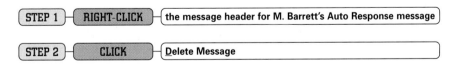

STEP 1 — RIGHT-CLICK — **the message header for M. Barrett's Auto Response message**

STEP 2 — CLICK — **Delete Message**

The message is moved to the Trash folder. When you no longer want the messages available for review, you should empty the Trash folder. If you are not sure what is stored in the Trash folder, it is a good idea to open it and view the contents.

MENU TIP

You can delete a selected message by clicking the Delete Message command on the Edit menu or by right-clicking a message header in the Message List pane and then clicking Delete Message. You also can delete a selected message by pressing the Delete key on the keyboard.

MOUSE TIP

You can click the Delete button on the Navigation toolbar to delete a selected message.

To open and then empty the Trash folder:

The message is deleted (or removed permanently) from the Trash folder. Next, you will delete the message you originally sent to M. Barrett. This time, you will empty the Trash folder without opening it first. To delete the original message to M. Barrett:

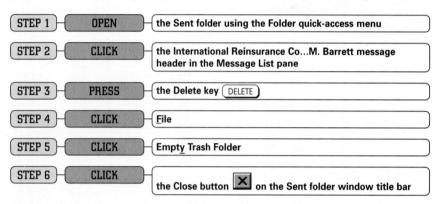

Now that you have completed the cycle of composing, sending, receiving, and deleting e-mail messages, it is time to consider some e-mail security and privacy issues.

3.k Recognizing E-Mail Security and Privacy Issues

Be aware that unethical Internet users may attempt to intercept your e-mail in search of sensitive information like passwords, credit card numbers, or intimate personal information. To protect your privacy, your ISP mail server stores your e-mail messages in a file that only you (and the system administrator) can open. That prevents other people from reading your e-mail. For further security, you can use encryption software to scramble and unscramble e-mail messages in transit.

You also should be aware that computer viruses can be transmitted over the Internet via e-mail messages. A computer virus is a set of instructions that can "infect" the memory or hard drive of your computer and damage files or destroy data. If you open an infected message, the virus can be transferred to your computer system. For that reason, it is a good idea to install on your computer antivirus software, which will automatically scan your computer memory and hard drives for viruses each time you turn on the computer. When a virus is detected, the antivirus software alerts you and provides a way to remove the virus. To find out more about computer viruses and antivirus software, see your instructor, current issues of popular computer magazines, or computer software vendors in your area.

3.1 Using Netiquette

The etiquette, or behavioral guidelines, for communicating with others on the Internet is called "Netiquette." Because the Internet is a cooperative effort, all users should try to be good Internet "citizens" by following appropriate Netiquette guidelines when sending e-mail, participating in newsgroups, or taking part in online chat groups.

Table 3-2 describes appropriate Netiquette for Internet communications.

TABLE 3-2

SITUATION	NETIQUETTE GUIDELINE
E-mail messages	Think twice about your message content before sending it; usually, you cannot "unsend" an e-mail message once it has been transmitted.
	Remember that e-mail messages can be easily circulated to others electronically or in printed copy.
	Even if you delete an e-mail message on your computer, it still may be stored on the ISP mail server or at its destination.
	E-mail messages can be subpoenaed in legal actions.
	Be cautious with humor; a message that is humorous to you might be confusing or offensive to someone else.
	Do not forward "junk mail" messages to other people.
	Use emoticons, or "smileys," to indicate emotions. For example, :-) indicates cheerfulness, while :-(indicates displeasure. (Turn the page 90 degrees clockwise to "read" the emotion.)
E-mail, newsgroups, chat	Avoid typing your message text in all capital letters WHICH INDICATES SHOUTING to the recipient.
	Degrading, offensive, and insulting comments are always inappropriate.
	Exchanging sarcasm and criticism—"flames"—can escalate into a "flame war," which can be ugly and nonproductive.
Newsgroups	Never post unsolicited advertising to newsgroups. Soliciting business by posting advertising to newsgroups is inappropriate and likely will result in flames sent to you and to your ISP.

Using appropriate Netiquette and being a good Internet citizen is a serious matter. Behaving inappropriately can lead to public criticism posted to newsgroups and possible loss of ISP services.

3.m Participating in Mailing Lists

Mailing lists are computer discussion groups that use e-mail to communicate about topics of special interest, like hobbies and professional associations. To participate in a mailing list, you must "subscribe" to the list. Subscribing to a mailing list simply means adding your name to the list of people receiving e-mail on the topic.

Computers called **list servers** manage mailing lists. To subscribe to a mailing list, you must know the name of the list and the e-mail address of the list server. One way to find a mailing list is to use an Internet search engine to search for mailing lists of interest. One specialized search engine for finding mailing lists is called Liszt. (You will learn more about search engines in Chapter 4.)

After you find the name of a mailing list and the list server address of the list you wish to participate in, simply send an e-mail message as follows:

Mail To: list server address

Subject: leave this blank

Message In the message area type the word "subscribe," press the spacebar, type the name of the list, press the spacebar, and type your User name. The list server will capture your e-mail address automatically.

To post a message to the participants in the mailing list, you must know the list-contents address or the address where the postings are stored. The list-contents address is shown when you use the Liszt search engine to located mailing lists. When you want to stop participating in a mailing list, send an e-mail message to the list server with the word "unsubscribe," the name of the list, and your User name.

To close the Navigator window:

STEP 1 — CLICK the application Close button ☒ on the Netscape title bar

Summary

> Sending e-mail messages is one of the most popular ways to use the Internet because you can send message anywhere at any time of the day or night; they can be delivered cheaply and quickly; and they generate quick replies.

> The Inbox window, the primary Messenger window, contains a menu bar, the Navigation and Location toolbars, the Folder quick-access menu, the Message Center button, the Message List pane, the Message pane, the Message pane control icon, and the status bar. The status bar contains the Security indicator, the Progress bar, and the Component Bar.

> E-mail addresses consist of a user name, the @ symbol, and the host name of the ISP mail computer.

> You store e-mail addresses in the Personal Address Book.

> You enter e-mail messages in the Composition window along with the e-mail address of the person who will receive the e-mail message.

> It is good practice to spell-check an e-mail message before you send it.

> You will see a green arrow next to the Mailbox icon on the Component Bar when you have mail waiting at your ISP; you also can check for messages anytime using one of several methods.

> You can reply to or forward messages by selecting the message header in the Message List pane and clicking a button on the Navigation toolbar.

> After deleting an e-mail message from any of the mail folders, you also should empty the Trash folder.

> You can preview and print e-mail much as you would a document in a word processing program.

> E-mail can be a target for interception or unauthorized access because it may contain sensitive information.

> You should install antivirus software on your computer to protect against infection by viruses transmitted with application software or via e-mail.

> Netiquette refers to the behavioral guidelines for being a good Internet citizen.

> Mailing lists are computer discussion groups that use e-mail to communicate about topics of special interest, like hobbies and professional associations.

SCANS

Commands Review

ACTION	MENU BAR	SHORTCUT MENU	MOUSE	KEYBOARD
Add an e-mail address to the Address Book	Message, Add to Address Book	Right-click message header, click Add to Address Book		ALT+M, A
Check for incoming messages	File, Get Messages		Get Msg	ALT+F, T CTRL+T
Close the Mail window	File, Close		X	ALT+F, C CTRL+W
Compose a new message	Message, New Message		New Msg	ALT+M, N CTRL+M
Delete a message	Edit, Delete Message	Right-click message header in Message List pane, click Delete Message	Delete	ALT+E, D DELETE key
Empty the Trash folder	File, Empty Trash Folder			Select item, ALT+F, Y DELETE key
Open the Address Book window	Communicator, Address Book		Address	ALT+C, A CTRL+SHIFT+2
Open the Inbox window	Communicator, Messenger Mailbox			ALT+C, M CTRL+2
Open the Navigator browser	Start, Programs, Netscape Communicator, Navigator		Netscape Communicator desktop shortcut	
Open various mail folders			Folder quick-access menu	
Preview a message	File, Print Preview			ALT+F, V
Print a message	File, Print			ALT+F, P CTRL+P
Reply to a selected message	Message, Reply, Reply to Sender or Reply to Sender and all Recipients	Right-click message header in Message List pane, click Reply	Reply	ALT+M, R CTRL+R CTRL+SHIFT+R
Send a message	File, Send Now		Send	ALT+F, D CTRL+ENTER

Concepts Review

Circle the correct answer.

1. Which of the following is not an advantage of using e-mail?
   [a] You can transmit messages at any time of the day or night.
   [b] You usually get quick replies.
   [c] You must pay for a long-distance call.
   [d] You can communicate in an efficient and cost-effective way.

2. You can get information about your current download of e-mail messages from the:
   [a] Progress bar.
   [b] Security indicator.
   [c] Component Bar.
   [d] Inbox.

3. The simplest way to locate someone's e-mail address is to:
   [a] Use the search engine Liszt.
   [b] Ask your ISP server.
   [c] Ask that person.
   [d] Use the Location toolbar.

4. Which of the following folders does not appear in the Folder quick-access menu list?
   [a] Sent.
   [b] Inbox.
   [c] Trash.
   [d] Saved.

5. You view the body of a selected e-mail message in the:
[a] Message pane.
[b] Message List pane.
[c] status bar.
[d] Inbox folder.

6. The Address Book is a:
[a] list of addresses from every e-mail you receive.
[b] list of e-mail addresses you store for future use.
[c] file that contains your personal information, such as credit card numbers.
[d] text file with your company name and address that is appended to your messages.

7. A signature file is:
[a] an ASCII file that contains your e-mail message.
[b] a text file that can be attached to your e-mail message.
[c] a file that your ISP needs to verify your signature.
[d] a text file with your name and company name that is appended to your messages.

8. A green arrow to the left of the Mailbox icon means that you:
[a] are connected to the Internet.
[b] have received a new message.
[c] can compose an e-mail message.
[d] have spell-checked your entire message.

9. Before you print an e-mail message you should:
[a] save the message.
[b] spell-check the message.
[c] reply to the message.
[d] preview the message.

10. Computers that manage mailing lists are called:
[a] signature files.
[b] list servers.
[c] flames.
[d] Liszt.

Circle (T) if the statement is true or (F) if the statement is false.

1. (T) (F) You can permanently delete messages by emptying the Sent folder.

2. (T) (F) The Progress bar identifies a secure or insecure transmission.

3. (T) (F) The following is a valid e-mail address: svanderbilt@century.com.

4. (T) (F) You should never format your e-mail messages as HTML text.

5. (T) (F) It is a good practice to check the spelling of a message before you send it.

6. (T) (F) E-mail messages are transmitted over the Internet as unformatted text known as ASCII text.

7. (T) (F) You can stop the transmission of an e-mail message before it's complete.

8. (T) (F) Messenger will check your ISP mail server only once each day for new incoming messages.

9. (T) (F) If you post unsolicited business advertising to Newsgroups, you will be rewarded with a large volume of new business.

10. (T) (F) Mailing lists are computer discussion groups that use e-mail to communicate about topics.

Fill in the blank to complete the sentence.

1. If you do not know what type of e-mail someone likes to receive, you should format your message as _____.

2. To always skip over a "misspelled" word, click the _____ button.

3. Messages you send are stored in the _____ folder.

4. To check for incoming messages, click the _____ button on the Navigation toolbar.

5. You can respond to an e-mail message quickly by clicking the _____ button on the Navigation toolbar.

6. A computer _____ is a set of instructions that can "infect" your computer's memory or hard drive and damage or destroy data.

7. The behavioral guidelines for communicating with others on the Internet is called _____.

8. Typing a message in all capital letters indicates _____ to the recipient.

9. A(n) _____ is a highly sarcastic and critical e-mail response sent to you and your ISP.

10. To participate in a mailing list, you must _____ to the list.

Case Problems

PROBLEM 1

As the International Reinsurance Conference draws nearer, you need to let J. Shaffer, the general branch manager of WorldWide Insurance Brokers, know how many branch managers will be attending. His e-mail address is jshaffer@notesgw.course.com.

1. Add J. Shaffer's e-mail address to your Personal Address Book. Include the comment that the regular work schedule is Tuesday through Saturday.

2. Compose an e-mail message to J. Shaffer. Use the address book to select the addresses for the Mail To: text box. Enter an appropriate message that indicates all the branch managers will attend the International Reinsurance Conference. Find out if you need to make any other arrangements for the conference. Spell-check your message before you send it.

3. Check for any new messages. Preview and print the response you receive from Joseph Shaffer.

PROBLEM 2

Select the message you created in Problem 1 from the Sent folder, then preview and print the message. Delete that message from the Sent folder. Delete the message you received from J. Shaffer, then empty the Trash folder.

PROBLEM 3

J. Shaffer's new work schedule is Monday through Wednesday, Friday, and Saturday. You need to revise the information on his address card in your Personal Address Book. Select his name in the Address Book list, click the Card Properties command on the Edit menu, change the information in the Notes: text box, then click OK.

PROBLEM 4: HELP

If you are using a dial-up connection, you sometimes might want to look at messages you have received without actually connecting to your ISP. Use the online Help system to find out how to do this.

1. Start Netscape.

2. Use the Help Options on the Help menu to access Communicator's online Help system.

3. Click the Sending and receiving e-mail link on the Contents page.

4. On a piece of paper, explain how to open your Inbox without connecting to your ISP.

PROBLEM 5: COMMUNICATE YOUR IDEAS

Learning to communicate effectively and appropriately over the Internet is important. Prepare a short presentation on Netiquette. Explain what behavior is considered appropriate and inappropriate for Internet communication. Discuss why and give examples.

SCANS

Quick Start for Browsing the Web with Navigator

> *"*
>
> *Although we are only a company of 20 people, our Web site gets over 1,000 hits each day. This exposure to a wide variety of people allows us to promote our company. Through links on our site to other sites, we are also able to help create a network of people who share the same interests that we do.*
>
> *"*

Kija Kim
president

Harvard Design and Mapping Co., Inc.
Cambridge, MA

Harvard Design and Mapping Company provides geographic information systems (GIS), mapping integration, and technology solutions to end users in corporations and government agencies.

Chapter Overview:

In Chapter 3, you learned to use the Internet's e-mail services and the Messenger application. In this chapter you will learn how to use an important subset of the Internet, the World Wide Web. You can use the World Wide Web to search for specific information, shop for and purchase goods and services, make travel arrangements, review popular entertainment venues, play games, get vendor product support, and much more. The World Wide Web is a network of special computers, called **Web servers**, that store files known as Web pages. In this chapter you will learn how to connect, or link, to a Web server. Then you will learn how to display a Web page on your computer. You also will learn how to use directories and search engines to find Web pages. Finally, you will learn how to save and print a Web page.

SNAPSHOT

In this chapter you will learn to:

> **Understand the World Wide Web**

> **Use the Online Companion**

> **Use the Offline Companion**

> **Use directories and search engines**

> **Save a Web page**

> **Print a Web page**

> **Return to the default home page**

IN THIS BOOK

Before opening the Communicator application and beginning any activities in this chapter, you should connect to your ISP. If you do not have an ISP connection, you can use the Offline Companion, as explained later in this chapter. If you plan to use the Offline Companion, continue reading the text until you come to the section "Using the Offline Companion." Then follow the steps as indicated.

4.a Understanding the World Wide Web

Before learning how to use the World Wide Web, or WWW, you need to become familiar with some of the basic terms related to it. A collection of Web pages on a Web server is often called a **Web site**. The primary page at a Web site is called the **home page**. Web pages are created with a special programming language called **Hypertext Markup Language**, or **HTML**. (You will learn more about creating a Web page using HTML in Chapter 8.)

Web pages are multimedia files, which means they can contain text, graphics, video, and audio. In addition, they can contain **hypertext links** (usually called simply **links**), which, when clicked, show other areas of the same Web page, load other Web pages at the same Web site, or load a Web page from a different Web site. Links create a "web" of connections between Web pages, allowing you to move quickly from one Web page to another. You can spot the links on a Web page because they usually are identified by colored and underlined text. Pictures also are used as links. You will have a chance to experiment with links later in this chapter.

Clicking links and moving from one Web page to another is known as **browsing** the Web. The application that you use to browse the Web, in this case, Navigator, is called a **browser**. Web pages are transmitted to your computer via a special communication protocol, or set of rules, called **Hypertext Transfer Protocol**, or **HTTP**. Each Web page on the World Wide Web is identified by a special location code called a **Uniform Resource Locator**, or **URL**. For example, the URL for the Netscape Web page is:

```
http://home.netscape.com/
```

where "http://" is the communication protocol and syntax, and "home.netscape.com/" is the name of the Web server containing the Web page. The Netscape home page URL is a simple one. But as you will see when you begin browsing the Web, some URLs are lengthy and contain additional information about the path and the filename of the Web page.

Before you begin,

| STEP 1 | START | Navigator from the Start menu or from the Communicator desktop icon |

If the default home page is the Welcome to Netscape page, your screen should look similar to Figure 4-1 (after you connect to your ISP and start Navigator). In the rest of this chapter, you will learn the basics about using Navigator to browse the Web. You will learn more details about the Navigator window in Chapter 5.

IN THIS BOOK

This book assumes that the default home page is the Netscape home page. However, many schools and businesses have a special page as their default home page. As a result, your default home page may differ from Figure 4-1. You will learn how to move to a different page in the next section.

FIGURE 4-1

1. Location text box

IN THIS BOOK

The World Wide Web is an ever changing environment, where pages are added and modified constantly. For that reason, the Web page illustrations in this book may not be identical to the Web pages you see in the hands-on activities.

4.b Using the Online Companion

The **Online Companion** is a Web site maintained by Course Technology, the publisher of this book. You will use the Online Companion as the starting point for your Web browsing in this chapter. If you are connected to your ISP, follow the steps below to load the Online Companion Web page. If you are not connected to an ISP, read the rest of the section but do not actually perform the steps. Then continue with the next section, "Using the Offline Companion."

MENU TIP

You can click the Open Page command on the File menu to enter a URL.

IN THIS BOOK

When you start Navigator, the Location toolbar contains the Location: text box. As you load other Web pages, the name "Netsite:" sometimes replaces the name "Location:" for this text box. In either case, the text box shows the URL for the current Web page. For consistency, the hands-on activities in this book refer to the text box as the "Location: text box."

Also, be careful to enter a URL exactly as it is shown in the text when instructed to do so.

> **MOUSE TIP**
>
> You can select all or part of the current URL in the Location: text box on the Location toolbar and replace it by typing a new URL.

To load the Online Companion if you are connected to an ISP:

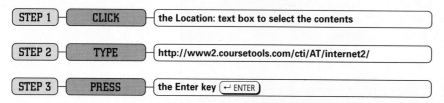

STEP 1 — CLICK — the Location: text box to select the contents

STEP 2 — TYPE — http://www2.coursetools.com/cti/AT/internet2/

STEP 3 — PRESS — the Enter key (↵ ENTER)

Navigator communicates with the Web server where the Online Companion is stored, and the process of **loading,** or transmitting, a copy of the Online Companion Web page begins.

Notice that the Stop button on the Navigation toolbar is red and that the Netscape icon to the right of the Stop button is animated, indicating transmission of the Web page is in progress. When the Web page is completely downloaded, the Stop button becomes inactive and the Netscape icon is no longer animated.

During the transmission process, the Status message field on the status bar at the bottom of the Navigator window contains a message about the progress of the transmission. When the Web page has been completely transmitted, the message "Document: Done" appears in the Status message field. Also, during the transmission process, the Progress bar to the left of the Status message field is animated, illustrating the progress of the transmission.

After the Online Companion Web page has been completely loaded, your screen should look similar to Figure 4-2.

FIGURE 4-2

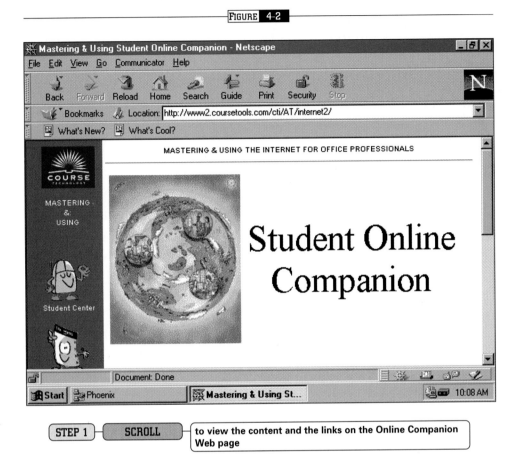

STEP 1 — SCROLL — to view the content and the links on the Online Companion Web page

If you are connected to an ISP and have loaded the Online Companion Web page, you can skip the next section and move ahead to "Using Directories and Search Engines." If you are not connected to an ISP and plan to use the Offline Companion, continue with the next section.

4.c Using the Offline Companion

If you do not have access to the Internet via an ISP, you can complete the hands-on activities in the remaining chapters by using the Offline Companion. The Offline Companion provides the same Web pages and links as the Online Companion. Your instructor will tell you where your Offline Companion files are located—on a network drive, a CD-ROM drive, or your computer's hard drive. If necessary, your instructor will help you download the Offline Companion files to your own computer. Check with your instructor to make sure the Offline Companion is properly installed on your computer. Then you can load the Offline Companion in Navigator as follows:

STEP 1 — CLICK — File

STEP 2 — CLICK — Open Page

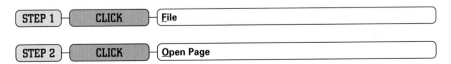

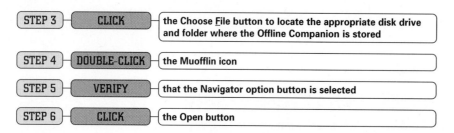

STEP 3	CLICK	the Choose File button to locate the appropriate disk drive and folder where the Offline Companion is stored
STEP 4	DOUBLE-CLICK	the Muofflin icon
STEP 5	VERIFY	that the Navigator option button is selected
STEP 6	CLICK	the Open button

The Offline Companion loads. Except for the location or path of the Offline Companion in the Location: text box, your screen should look similar to Figure 4-3.

FIGURE 4-3

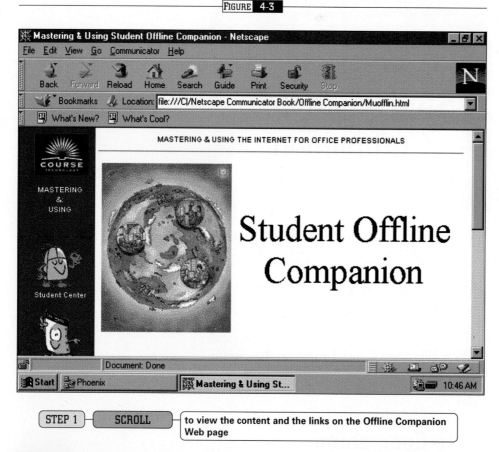

| STEP 1 | SCROLL | to view the content and the links on the Offline Companion Web page |

4.d Using Directories and Search Engines

Directories are special Web sites that maintain an index of other Web sites by category, such as business or entertainment. You can search a directory's index by a keyword or a phrase for a specific Web site or click multiple links to move from Web site to Web site through a specific category to locate a desired Web site. When you do a keyword search in a directory, you are searching only the directory's index, not the entire WWW. Popular directories include Yahoo!, Galaxy, and Magellan Internet Guide.

Search engines are special Web sites that maintain an index of Web pages from the entire WWW. You can search this index by keyword or by phrase to find a specific Web page. You will learn more about search engines in Chapter 5. Popular search engines include Alta Vista and WebCrawler. For the activities in this chapter, you will use the search engine included in the Online and Offline Companions.

Search engines can be powerful tools that help you gather information quickly. For example, suppose a vice president of your company, J. Hillsdale, has asked you to locate a company that can provide special training classes in the latest version of your office suite software. In the next set of steps, you will use the Online or Offline Companion search engine to search the World Wide Web for companies that can provide those services. You will begin by searching for the keywords "software training."

> **IN THIS BOOK**
>
> If you are using the Offline Companion, the results you see on your screen may vary from the figures in this chapter, which were created using the Online Companion.

To search for Web pages containing the keywords "software training":

STEP 1	SCROLL	to view the Internet Search: text box
STEP 2	CLICK	inside the Internet Search: text box to position the insertion point
STEP 3	TYPE	software training

Your screen should look similar to Figure 4-4.

FIGURE 4-4

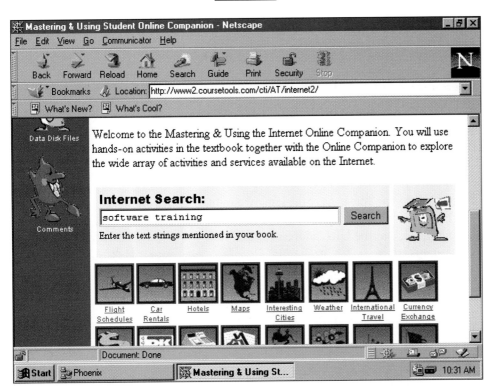

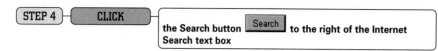

STEP 4 — CLICK the Search button [Search] to the right of the Internet Search text box

In a few seconds, the Internet Search Results page for "software training" loads. Your screen should look similar to Figure 4-5.

FIGURE 4-5

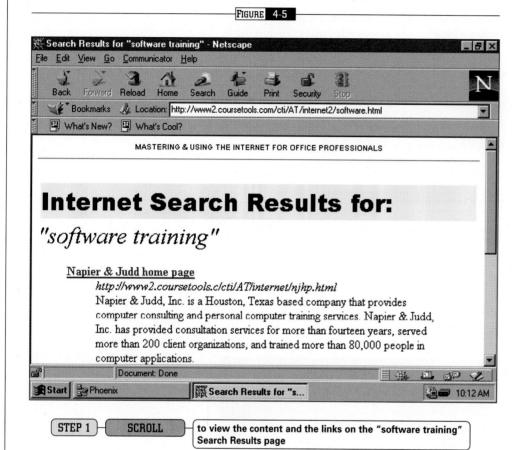

STEP 1 — SCROLL to view the content and the links on the "software training" Search Results page

The search engine found three Web pages in its index that contain the keyword phrase "software training." Notice that the title for each Web page appears in a different color from the text and is underlined. As you learned earlier in this chapter, text that appears underlined and in a different color on a Web page is a hypertext link, or link, to another area on the same Web page, a different Web page at the same Web site, or a Web page at a different Web site. When you place your mouse pointer on a link, it changes shape to a hand with a pointing finger, and the URL address for that link appears in the Status message field on the status bar.

QUICK TIP

Hypertext links can be text or graphics. If you position your mouse pointer on text or graphics and the mouse pointer changes shape to a hand with a pointing finger, the text or graphic is a hypertext link.

To use the link to load the Napier & Judd home page:

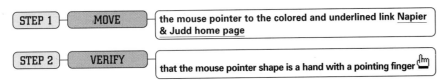

STEP 1 — MOVE — the mouse pointer to the colored and underlined link **Napier & Judd home page**

STEP 2 — VERIFY — that the mouse pointer shape is a hand with a pointing finger 👆

Your screen should look similar to Figure 4-6.

FIGURE 4-6

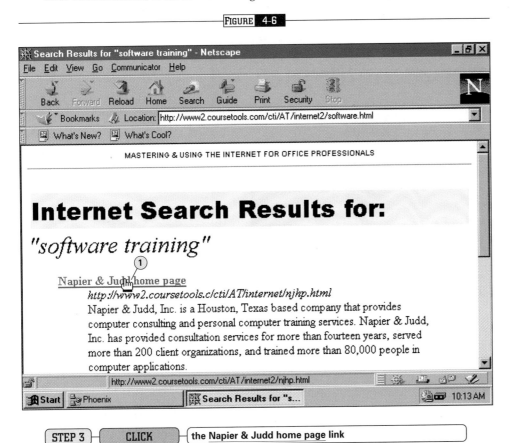

1. Mouse pointer

STEP 3 — CLICK — the Napier & Judd home page link

The Napier & Judd home page appears. Your screen should look similar to Figure 4-7.

FIGURE 4-7

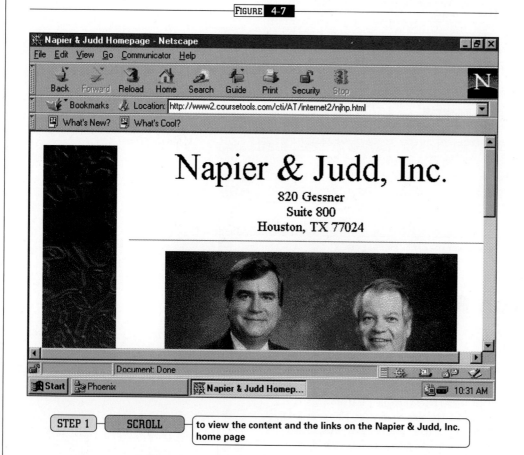

STEP 1 ── SCROLL ── to view the content and the links on the Napier & Judd, Inc. home page

The Napier & Judd, Inc. home page contains links to three other Web pages at the same Web site: Education, Textbooks, and Consulting & Programming. Because you are looking for information on training services, click the Education link. That link should display information about Napier & Judd's training services.

To continue the research:

STEP 1 ── MOVE ── the mouse pointer to the Education link [Education]

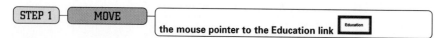

The mouse pointer shape changes to a hand with a pointing finger, indicating that it is positioned over a link.

STEP 2 ── CLICK ── [Education]

The Napier & Judd Education Web page appears, with information about the company's education services.

STEP 3 ── SCROLL ── to view the content and links on the Napier & Judd, Inc. Education Web page

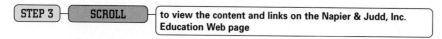

MENU TIP

You can also use the mouse to load a new Web page in a new Navigator window by right-clicking a hypertext link and then clicking the Open in New Window command.

Each software title listed on the page is a link to another Web page that provides more information about training classes for that particular program.

Now that you have found the information you need, you can save or print the Web page. You will learn how to do both in the next section.

4.e Saving a Web Page

To provide the company president with information about Napier & Judd's training classes, you decide to keep a copy of the Web page. You can save the Web page to a disk and print it later, or you can print it now without saving it. You decide to save the Web page for future reference and to print a copy now.

When you save a Web page, you can save it as a text file (without formatting) that you can then open in a word processing application, like Word 97. You can also save a Web page as an HTML document that retains its original text formatting. You then can open the HTML document from your disk in either a browser application, like Navigator, or an HTML editor, like Netscape Composer.

To save the Napier & Judd Education Web page as a text document:

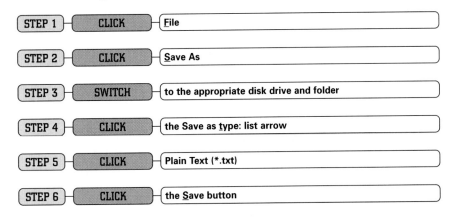

STEP 1 — CLICK — File

STEP 2 — CLICK — Save As

STEP 3 — SWITCH — to the appropriate disk drive and folder

STEP 4 — CLICK — the Save as type: list arrow

STEP 5 — CLICK — Plain Text (*.txt)

STEP 6 — CLICK — the Save button

The Napier & Judd Education Web page is saved as a text document.

4.f Printing a Web Page

Before you print a Web page, you might want to preview it. That way, you can adjust margins and other print settings before you use the time and the paper it takes to actually print the Web page. The previewing and printing process for a Web page is like previewing and printing any Windows application document. To preview the Web page:

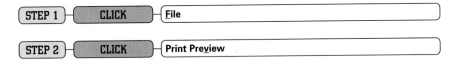

STEP 1 — CLICK — File

STEP 2 — CLICK — Print Preview

The current Web page appears in the Print Preview window. The Web page preview looks fine, so you can go ahead and print it. To print the Web page:

STEP 3 ┤ CLICK the Print button [Print...] on the Print Preview toolbar

The Print Preview window closes, and the Print dialog box opens. Note that before you print a Web page, you may want to change some of the Web page setup options like margins, print a document header, print the Web page URL, or change the text color to black. Click the Page Setup command on the File menu to view Web page setup options.

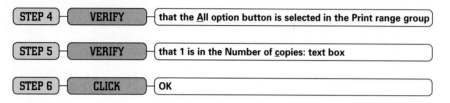
STEP 4 ┤ VERIFY that the All option button is selected in the Print range group

STEP 5 ┤ VERIFY that 1 is in the Number of copies: text box

STEP 6 ┤ CLICK OK

A copy of the Napier & Judd Education Services Web page prints.

4.g Returning to the Default Home Page

It is easy to become disoriented and forget your starting point when you browse the Web by following several links to different Web pages. One way to return to your starting point is to reload the default home page.

IN THIS BOOK

Remember that this text assumes the Netscape home page is the default home page. However, you can easily change your default home page by changing the URL entered in the Home Page Location: text box in the Preferences dialog box. To open this dialog box, use the Preferences command on the Edit menu. Do *not* change your default home page unless your instructor gives you permission.

To reload the default Netscape home page:

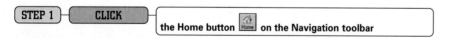
STEP 1 ┤ CLICK the Home button [Home] on the Navigation toolbar

In a few seconds, the Netscape home page appears. Because you have found all the information you need on software training, you can close the Navigator application.

STEP 2 ┤ CLICK the Close button [X] on the Navigator title bar

Summary

> A collection of Web pages on a Web server is called a Web site. The primary page on a Web site is called the home page. Web pages are created with a special programming language called Hypertext Markup Language, or HTML. Hypertext links, commonly called links, connect Web pages and allow you to move from one Web page to another. Web pages are transmitted via a special communication protocol called Hypertext Transfer Protocol, or HTTP.

> The Online Companion is a special Web page you can use as a starting point for browsing the Web.

> The Offline Companion provides access to Web pages and links without an actual connection to the Internet.

> Directories and search engines are special Web sites that provide tools for locating Web sites or specific Web pages.

> You can save a Web page for future reference as a text file.

> You can easily preview and print a Web page.

> To return to your starting point when you are browsing the Web, reload the default home page.

Commands Review

ACTION	MENU BAR	SHORTCUT MENU	MOUSE	KEYBOARD
Change the page setup before you print a Web page	File, Page Setup			ALT+F, G
Load a new Web page using the mouse		Right-click a hypertext link, click Open in New window	Click a hypertext link	
Load a Web page as a local file	File, Open Page			ALT+F, O CTRL+O
Load a Web page by typing the URL				Type the URL in the Location: text box
Preview a Web page before you print it	File, Print Preview			ALT+F, V
Print a Web page	File, Print		Print Print	ALT+F, P
Save a Web page	File, Save As	Right-click a hypertext link, click Save Link As		ALT+F, S
Return to the default home page	Go, Home		Home	ALT+G, H
Load the Online Companion				www2.Coursetools. com/cti/AT/internet2/
Load the Offline Companion	File, Open Page			

Concepts Review

Circle the correct answer.

1. The World Wide Web is a:

[a] special communication protocol.

[b] network of special computers called Web servers.

[c] special location code.

[d] special programming language.

2. To move to from one Web page to another Web page at a different Web site, you:

[a] click a hypertext link.

[b] scroll the screen.

[c] load the Online Companion.

[d] close the Web page you are viewing.

3. Hypertext Markup Language is a special:

[a] code that identifies a picture on the World Wide Web.

[b] picture you click to load another Web page.

[c] communication protocol for the World Wide Web.

[d] markup language used to create Web pages.

4. The primary page at a Web site is called a:

[a] hypertext link.

[b] Uniform Resource Locator.

[c] home page.

[d] search engine.

5. A URL is a:

[a] special location code.

[b] communication protocol.

[c] default home page.

[d] name of a Web server.

6. Web pages are transmitted to your computer via a special set of rules, called:

[a] URL.

[b] HTML.

[c] WWW.

[d] HTTP.

7. A Web site that maintains an index of other Web sites by category is called a:

[a] search engine.

[b] directory.

[c] browser.

[d] Web server.

8. Search engines:

[a] link pages.

[b] define your default home page.

[c] locate Web pages on the WWW.

[d] save Web pages for future reference.

9. Before you print a Web page, you should:

[a] preview it.

[b] save it.

[c] record its URL.

[d] make it your home page.

10. Reload the default home page to:

[a] go back one page.

[b] move forward one page.

[c] save a Web page.

[d] return to your starting point.

Circle [T] if the statement is true or [F] if the statement is false.

1. [T] [F] Web servers store files known as Web pages.

2. [T] [F] The primary Web page at a Web site is called the home page.

3. [T] [F] The correct format for a URL is http://home.netscape.com/.

4. [T] [F] Hypertext links must be text.

5. [T] [F] The WWW is an ever changing environment in which pages are added and modified constantly.

6. [T] [F] You can search for a specific Web site with a directory.

7. [T] [F] When you position the mouse pointer on a link, it changes to a red arrow.

8. [T] [F] You cannot stop the transmission of a Web page once you initiate the process.

9. [T] [F] A Web page can be saved as a text file or a formatted HTML document.

10. [T] [F] There is no reason to preview a Web page before you print it.

Fill in the blank to complete the sentence.

1. A collection of Web pages on a Web server is called a(n) _____.

2. _____ are multimedia files, which can contain text, graphics, video, and audio.

3. Clicking links and moving from one Web page to another is known as _____.

4. When the Stop button on the Navigation toolbar is red and the Netscape icon is animated, a Web page is _____ .

5. _____ and _____ are tools available on the WWW to help you find Web pages.

6. You search either a directory index or a search engine index by a(n) _____ to find a specific Web page.

7. You can save a Web page to a(n) _____ to retain its original text formatting.

8. To print a Web page, you can click the _____ button on the Print Preview toolbar.

9. To load the default home page, click the _____ button on the Navigation toolbar.

10. When you point to a link, the mouse pointer changes to a(n) _____ .

Case Problems

PROBLEM 1

Complete this problem using the Online or Offline Companion.

You are the assistant to Sally Nollon, the manager of the IS department in your company. She asks you to find an online bookstore that has a catalog of technical books.

Start Navigator, load the Online or Offline Companion Web page, and use the search engine to search for "online bookstores." When the list of possible online bookstores appears, click the Amazon.com link. Review the Amazon.com home page, save it as a text file, and print it. Reload the default home page, preview and print it. Close Navigator.

PROBLEM 2

Complete this case problem using your ISP connection and the Internet.

The sales manager of your company plans to give away sports merchandise as special prizes at the upcoming sales meeting. It's your job to help by locating an online catalog for merchandise sold by a national football, hockey, basketball, baseball, or soccer league.

Start Navigator. Enter your best guess for the appropriate URL in the Location: text box and load the home page. Print the home page, then find the link for gift merchandise and click it. Print the merchandise Web page. Reload the default home page and close Navigator.

PROBLEM 3: HELP

As the associate researcher for a business magazine, you are responsible for verifying all URLs that are published as part of an article or advertisement. As Web browsing increases in popularity and the number of business sites is on the rise, you find that you spend several hours each day typing URLs to load Web pages. Your boss mentioned that you don't have to type the entire URL each time. You decide to check Navigator's online Help to find out more.

Start Navigator, then use the Help Contents command on the Help menu to open the online Help system. Click the Browsing the Web link, then locate the "Using a URL" subtopic in the "Links and URLs" topic. Read about entering partial URLs.

Write a paragraph that tells what parts of a URL Navigator will fill in for you. Give three examples of complete URLs and the partial URL you would have to type in the Location: box. Explain the advantage of this Netscape feature.

Using Navigator Features

"

The Internet is the first place I go for information. On the Internet I can comparison shop by viewing different company Web pages, find company e-mail addresses using the Web yellow pages, and buy gifts for my friends and family. Anything that you ever needed to know is on the Web.

"

Tom Kutter
consultant

Open Market, Inc.
Cambridge, MA

Open Market, Inc., is a provider of Internet software for business. Its products form the foundation for enterprise-wide applications and secure electronic commerce.

Chapter Overview:

Chapter 4 provided a quick introduction to the WWW. You learned how to use links to display Web pages in the Navigator browser and how to use a search engine to find Web pages based on specific keywords. As you will learn in this chapter, Navigator contains many features to help you find and load Web pages. You will start by learning more about the Navigator window. Then you'll learn several methods for loading Web pages and how to use special features like the Page Proxy. Finally, you will learn how security indicators can help you monitor security on the WWW.

SNAPSHOT

In this chapter you will learn to:

> Describe the components of the Navigator window

> Load Web pages

> Create bookmarks

> Work with Navigator shortcuts

> Customize the Personal toolbar

> Manage the toolbars

> Search the WWW with the Navigator Search page

> Use the Guide feature to find e-mail addresses and company information

> View security information

IN THIS CHAPTER

The activities in this chapter assume you are using the Online Companion. If you are using the Offline Companion, start Navigator and load the Offline Companion. Then load the Napier & Judd, Inc. home page. (Review the steps in Chapter 4 to load the Offline Companion and search for the Napier & Judd, Inc. home page, if necessary.) In the hands-on activities in this chapter, substitute the Napier & Judd, Inc. home page for the Course Technology home page when creating bookmarks.

5.a Describing the Components of the Navigator Window

In this section, you will examine the major elements of the Navigator window. Before you begin, you need to start Navigator:

STEP 1 — **START** — Navigator from the Start menu or the Communicator desktop icon

Figure 5-1 illustrates the components of the Navigator window.

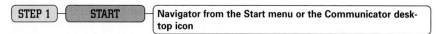
FIGURE 5-1

1. Title bar
2. Menu bar
3. Navigation toolbar
4. Location toolbar
5. Personal toolbar
6. Content area
7. Status line
8. Netsite or Location box
9. Progress bar
10. Status message area
11. Security indicator
12. Page Proxy icon
13. Bookmark QuickFile
14. Toolbar tabs
15. Netcenter menu
16. Page tab

TITLE BAR

The **title bar** contains the Navigator Control-menu icon and application name, the title of the current Web page, and the Navigator Minimize, Restore, and Close buttons.

MENU BAR

The **menu bar** contains the menu commands you use to perform specific tasks when viewing the Navigator window, such as opening a file from your hard disk or printing the current Web page.

NAVIGATION TOOLBAR

The **Navigation toolbar** contains buttons that provide shortcuts to frequently performed tasks, making it easier to move among Web pages.

LOCATION TOOLBAR

The **Location toolbar** contains the **Bookmark QuickFile** list, the **Page Proxy** icon, and the **Location box**. (The Location box is sometimes called the Netsite box, depending on what type of Web site you currently are connected to.) You can save a Web page uniform resource locator (URL) as a bookmark or reference that appears in the Bookmark QuickFile list. As you will learn later in this chapter, you can use the Bookmark QuickFile list and Page Proxy icon to create shortcuts to Web pages you use often. The **Personal toolbar** is a customizable toolbar to which you can add bookmarks for files and Web pages. You'll learn how to customize it later in this chapter.

STATUS LINE

The **Status line** displays information about the current Web page. The **Security indicator** (the open padlock icon) identifies whether the page being downloaded is a secure (encrypted) document. As a Web page loads, the **Progress bar** becomes animated to illustrate the progress of the downloading process. When you place the mouse pointer on a link in the current Web page, the URL associated with that link appears in the **status message area**. You are already familiar with the last element of the **Status line**, the Component Bar.

CONTENT AREA

The **content area** contains the current Web page. Vertical and horizontal scroll bars appear as necessary so you can scroll the entire Web page after it has been loaded.

NETCENTER MENU

The Netcenter menu contains shortcuts to different Web pages at Netscape's Web site. You can show or hide the Netcenter menu by clicking the Page tab. Also, the Netscape Web site now provides multiple layers of Web pages available at one time. To show or hide one of the layered Web pages, click the Page tab for the page. Figure 5-1 illustrates both the Netcenter menu and Page tabs.

QUICK TIP

Some pages are separated into segments called **frames**, with each frame containing a separate Web page. Often the frame boundaries can be sized with the mouse. You select a frame by clicking inside it. For more information on frames, see online Help.

5.b Loading Web Pages

To load a Web page, you must either know or find the URL. As you learned in Chapter 4, one way to find the URL for a Web page is to use a search engine or directory. If you are looking for the Web page for a particular company, you might find the URL in one of the company's newspaper, magazine, or television ads. Many companies now include their home page URL on their letterheads and business cards.

Sometimes you can load a Web page by guessing the page's URL and then typing your guess in the Location box. For example, suppose you want to review the home page for Course Technology, the publisher of this textbook. Often the descriptive host name portion of the URL contains a portion of the company name. Because the company name is Course Technology, it is reasonable to assume that part of the name is used to identify the host computer where the company's home page is stored. You might guess that "course" identifies the host computer and that it is in the commercial (.com) top-level domain. (You learned about domain names in Chapter 1.) That guess would produce the following URL for Course Technology:

http://www.course.com/

You can type a URL directly in the Location box by first selecting all or part of the current URL and replacing it with the new URL. To select the contents of the Location box:

| STEP 1 | CLICK | the Location box |

The URL for your default home page is selected in the Location box. Next, you can replace the complete URL or you can select just the portion of the URL you want to replace. If you omit the "http://" portion of the URL, Navigator will add it for you. To enter the URL for Course Technology:

| STEP 2 | TYPE | www.course.com |

| STEP 3 | PRESS | the Enter key (← ENTER) |

In a moment the Course Technology opening page loads. To load the home page:

| STEP 4 | CLICK | the Course Technology graphic to load the home page, if necessary |

MENU TIP

You can type a URL in the Open Page dialog box by first clicking the Open Page command on the File menu.

In a few seconds, the Course Technology home page appears. The URL is automatically extended to include the Web page's filename, "home.html." Your screen should look similar to Figure 5-2.

FIGURE 5-2

1. Complete URL including filename

To review the Course Technology home page:

| STEP 1 | SCROLL | the Course Technology home page to review the contents |

| STEP 2 | POSITION | the mouse pointer in different areas on the Course Technology home page to review the text or graphic links to other pages |

| STEP 3 | OBSERVE | that the URL for a text or graphic link appears in the Status message area on the status line when you position the mouse pointer on the link |

Note: Do not click on or "follow" other links at this time.

Following are other examples of identifying a URL by the name or common acronym for the company:

http://www.magnavox.com   Philips Magnavox
http://www.paramount.com   Paramount Studios
http://www.novell.com   Novell, Inc.
http://www.ge.com   General Electric
http://www.aetv.com   Arts & Entertainment Network

Web pages constantly are updated with new information. When you load a Web page that contains useful information, you may want to review the changes to that information on a regular basis. In the next section, you will learn how to save a Web page URL so you can load the page quickly without typing the URL.

IN THIS BOOK

If you are using the Offline Companion, begin the hands-on activities by substituting the Napier & Judd, Inc. home page for the Course Technology home page.

5.c Creating Bookmarks

If you like a certain Web page and want to revisit it, you can save its URL as a **bookmark**. For example, suppose you want to load the Course Technology home page frequently. You can create a bookmark that saves the Course Technology home page URL in a file on your hard disk. Then you can quickly load the Web page (without typing the URL in the Location box) by clicking it in the Bookmark QuickFile list.

The easiest way to add a bookmark is to drag the **Page Proxy** icon (located on the Location toolbar, as shown in Figure 5-1) onto the Bookmark button on the Location toolbar. To save the Course Technology home page URL as a bookmark using the Page Proxy icon:

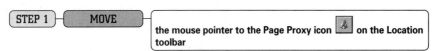
STEP 1 — MOVE — the mouse pointer to the Page Proxy icon on the Location toolbar

Your screen should look similar to Figure 5-3.

FIGURE 5-3

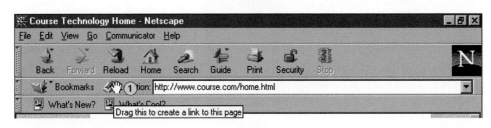

1. Mouse Pointer on Page Proxy icon

To add the Course Technology bookmark:

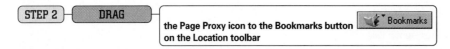
STEP 2 — DRAG — the Page Proxy icon to the Bookmarks button on the Location toolbar

The Bookmark QuickFile menu opens.

STEP 3 — RELEASE — the mouse button

The Course Technology bookmark is added to the Bookmark QuickFile list. To verify the addition of the Course Technology bookmark:

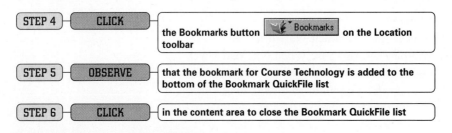
STEP 4 — CLICK — the Bookmarks button on the Location toolbar

STEP 5 — OBSERVE — that the bookmark for Course Technology is added to the bottom of the Bookmark QuickFile list

STEP 6 — CLICK — in the content area to close the Bookmark QuickFile list

MENU TIP

You create a bookmark by pointing to the Bookmarks command on the Communicator menu and then clicking Add Bookmark or by right-clicking a Web page in the content area (not on a link) and clicking Add Bookmark.

CAUTION

When you click in the Content area to close a menu, be careful not to click on a text or graphic link.

MANAGING YOUR BOOKMARKS

You can manage your saved bookmarks in the Bookmarks window just as you manage files in Windows Explorer. You display the Bookmarks window by pointing to the Bookmarks command on the Communicator menu and clicking Edit Bookmarks or by clicking the Bookmarks button on the Location toolbar and then clicking Edit Bookmarks. To display the Bookmarks window:

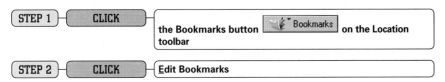

STEP 1 — CLICK — the Bookmarks button [Bookmarks] on the Location toolbar

STEP 2 — CLICK — Edit Bookmarks

The Bookmarks window opens. If many bookmarks are stored on your computer, the content of your Bookmarks window will vary substantially from Figure 5-4.

FIGURE 5-4

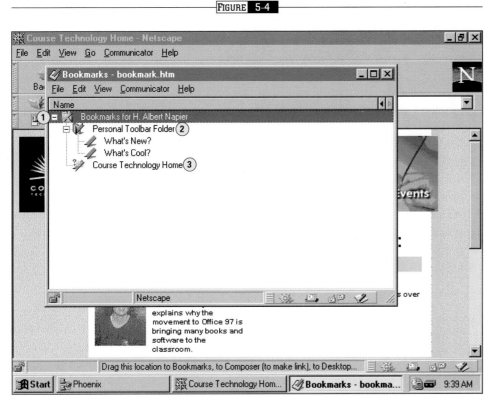

1. Main folder
2. Folder containing bookmarks on Personal toolbar
3. New bookmark for Course Technology Web page

Bookmarks are stored in folders. The folders are organized in a directory tree, just like the folders in Windows Explorer. The main folder is the "Bookmarks for" folder that appears at the top of the directory tree. When you save a bookmark, the Web page URL is stored in that folder by default. The other default folder is the Personal Toolbar folder, which contains bookmarks that appear as buttons on the Personal toolbar. You can create other folders with commands on the Bookmark window File menu. After you create a bookmark or a folder, you can move them using the drag-and-drop method, just as you move files and folders in Windows Explorer.

You also can expand and collapse the folders in the Bookmarks window to display or hide their contents just as you can in Windows Explorer. The Bookmarks window offers many opportunities for managing your bookmarks. For example, you can sort your bookmarks (i.e., view them in a different order) by using the commands on the Bookmarks window <u>V</u>iew menu. You also can save your bookmarks to a floppy disk and then import them into Navigator at another computer. To close the Bookmarks window and reload your default home page:

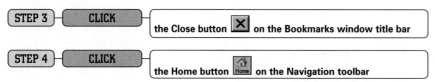

Your home page reloads. Now you can use the bookmark you just created to reload the Course Technology page. To use a bookmark to reload the Course Technology home page:

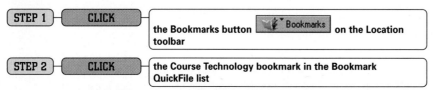

Once again, you see the Course Technology home page in the Navigator window.

5.d Working with Navigator Shortcuts

You can view previously loaded pages several different ways. When you first load a Web page, it is stored temporarily in your computer in **cache**, which is a temporary memory or hard-disk storage area. When you load a Web page by typing the URL, clicking a link, or clicking a bookmark, Navigator checks the Web server where the original Web page is stored to determine if any changes have been made since the Web page was loaded last. If the Web page has been changed, a fresh Web page is transmitted from the Web server. If there have been no changes, the Web page is retrieved from cache. For more detailed information on how Navigator uses cache, see online Help.

RELOADING WEB PAGES

Because previously loaded pages are stored in cache, you can click the <u>B</u>ack and <u>F</u>orward commands on the <u>G</u>o menu, or the Back and Forward buttons on the Navigation toolbar to reload them. You also can move quickly to a previously loaded page by clicking it in the list of recently loaded pages at the bottom of the <u>G</u>o menu. To access the <u>G</u>o menu:

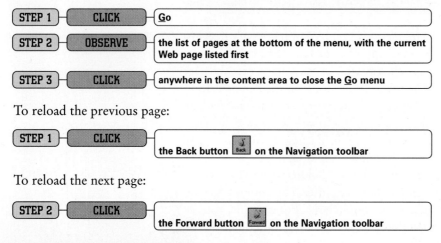

To reload the previous page:

To reload the next page:

VIEWING THE HISTORY LIST

A more detailed version of the list at the bottom of the <u>G</u>o menu is available in the History list. To view the History list, click <u>H</u>istory on the <u>C</u>ommunicator menu. The History window contains information about when the Web page was loaded and how many times it has been loaded. The first item in the list is the current Web page.

To display the History window:

STEP 1	CLICK	<u>C</u>ommunicator

STEP 2	CLICK	<u>H</u>istory

The History window opens. Your screen should look similar to Figure 5-5.

FIGURE 5-5

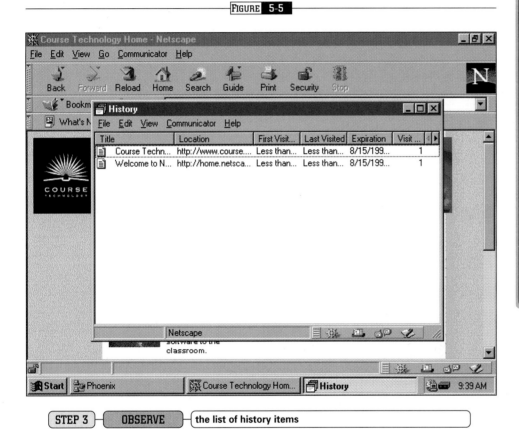

STEP 3	OBSERVE	the list of history items

You can reload any page in the History list by double-clicking it. To reload your default home page from the History list:

STEP 4	DOUBLE-CLICK	your default home page item in the History list

Your default home page reloads, and the History window is minimized to a button on the taskbar. To close the History window:

STEP 5	RIGHT-CLICK	the History window button on the taskbar

STEP 6	CLICK	<u>C</u>lose

QUICK TIP

You can select an item in the History list and then reload that page or create a bookmark for that page with commands on the History window <u>F</u>ile menu.

You can set a variety of options for how Navigator looks and how some of the features work by clicking the <u>P</u>references command on the <u>E</u>dit menu. For example, to specify the number of days an item remains in the History list, click Navigator in the Category list, then enter a number in the Pages in history expire after text box. A page that has been removed from the History list is said to have expired.

When you click a link to a Web page, that link changes color to indicate a "followed link," that is, a link you recently clicked. When an item is removed from the History list (or expires), all links to the page revert to their original color.

5.e Customizing the Personal Toolbar

The Personal toolbar allows you to create custom shortcuts to your favorite Web pages. You create such shortcuts by adding bookmarks, which are displayed on the Personal toolbar as buttons.

Suppose you want to add a bookmark to the Course Technology home page to your Personal toolbar.

QUICK TIP

The **What's New?** and **What's Cool?** buttons on the Personal toolbar appear by default and provide a built-in list of new and interesting Web pages provided by Navigator. Yours may look different from those shown in the illustrations.

| STEP 1 | RELOAD | the Course Technology home page |

To add a bookmark to the Personal toolbar using the Page Proxy icon and the mouse pointer:

STEP 2	MOVE	the mouse pointer to the Page Proxy icon
STEP 3	DRAG	the Page Proxy icon [icon] to a blank space on the Personal toolbar
STEP 4	RELEASE	the mouse button

A bookmark to the Course Technology home page appears on the Personal toolbar. Your screen should look similar to Figure 5-6.

FIGURE 5-6

1. Course Technology bookmark

Now that you have created the bookmark to the Course Technology home page on the Personal toolbar, reload the default home page and use the bookmark to reload the Course Technology home page.

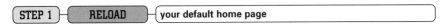

STEP 1 — RELOAD — your default home page

To load the Course Technology home page using the new bookmark on the Personal toolbar:

STEP 2 — CLICK — the Course Technology button on the Personal toolbar

The Course Technology home page reloads. Once you add a bookmark to the Personal toolbar, you can move it using the mouse or delete it using the Delete command on the Edit menu in the Bookmarks window. You will open the Edit menu in the Bookmarks window now. To open the Bookmarks window:

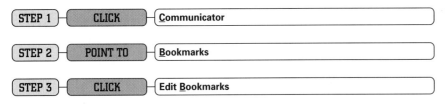

STEP 1 — CLICK — Communicator

STEP 2 — POINT TO — Bookmarks

STEP 3 — CLICK — Edit Bookmarks

The Bookmarks window opens. From here, you have several options. You can select a bookmark and drag it to a new location with the mouse pointer, or you can select it and delete it by pressing the DELETE key on the keyboard. You also can delete a bookmark by clicking the Delete Bookmark command on a shortcut menu. In the next set of steps you'll use the shortcut menu. To delete the Course Technology shortcut button from the Personal toolbar:

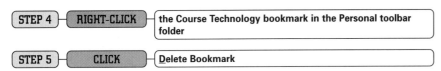

STEP 4 — RIGHT-CLICK — the Course Technology bookmark in the Personal toolbar folder

STEP 5 — CLICK — Delete Bookmark

To delete the Course Technology bookmark from the primary folder and the Bookmark QuickFile list using the keyboard:

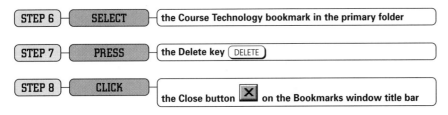

STEP 6 — SELECT — the Course Technology bookmark in the primary folder

STEP 7 — PRESS — the Delete key (DELETE)

STEP 8 — CLICK — the Close button [X] on the Bookmarks window title bar

Along with the Personal toolbar, Navigator's two other toolbars—the Navigation toolbar and the Location toolbar—provide many shortcuts to loading and navigating through Web pages. As you will see in the next section, sometimes you may want to hide or reposition those toolbars to provide more space in the content area.

QUICK TIP

For more drag-and-drop shortcuts in Navigator, see online Help.

5.f Managing the Toolbars

You can reposition, hide, or "unhide" the Navigation, Location, and Personal toolbars. For example, suppose you want to increase the vertical viewing space of the content area so you can view more of the current Web page without scrolling. You do that by hiding one or more of the toolbars. To hide a toolbar, simply click the toolbar tab. (The **toolbar tab** is the small vertical bar at the left end of a toolbar, as shown in Figure 5-1.) To hide the Personal toolbar:

| STEP 1 | CLICK | the Personal toolbar tab on the left end of the Personal toolbar |

The Personal toolbar is hidden and only the tab appears, allowing you to see more of the Web page in the content area. You can unhide the toolbar by clicking its tab again. Your screen should look similar to Figure 5-7.

FIGURE 5-7

1. Toolbar tabs
2. Tab for hidden toolbar

To show the Personal toolbar:

| STEP 2 | CLICK | the Personal toolbar tab below the Location toolbar |

The Personal toolbar reappears. In addition to hiding and unhiding toolbars, you can reposition them by dragging the toolbar tab to a new location. To reposition the Personal toolbar:

| STEP 1 | MOVE | the mouse pointer to the Personal toolbar tab |

| STEP 2 | DRAG | the Personal toolbar upward and drop it below the menu bar |

The Personal toolbar is now the first toolbar, directly below the menu bar. The Navigation toolbar moves down to become the second toolbar, and the Location toolbar is now the third toolbar.

| STEP 3 | CONTINUE | using the mouse to reposition the toolbars until they are in their original positions: Navigation toolbar, Location toolbar, and Personal toolbar |

To completely hide a toolbar and its tab, you can use the appropriate command on the <u>V</u>iew menu. Keep in mind that when you use a <u>V</u>iew menu command to hide a toolbar, you also must use a <u>V</u>iew menu command to show it.

In addition to shortcuts for loading Web pages and managing the toolbars, Navigator also provides a special Web page, called a search page, that contains lists of popular Web directories and search engines you can use to find information on the WWW. In the next section, you will load and review the Navigator search page.

5.g Searching the WWW with the Navigator Search Page

Because the WWW is so large, you often need to take advantage of special search tools called search engines and directories to find the information you need. For example, in Chapter 4 you used a search engine on the Online or Offline Companion Web page to find Web pages containing the keywords "software training." To use some of the Web's numerous other search engines and directories, you can click the Search button on the Navigation toolbar. To view the Navigator search page:

STEP 1 — CLICK — the Search button [Search] on the Navigation toolbar

In a few seconds, the Navigator search page loads. Your screen should look similar to Figure 5-8.

FIGURE 5-8

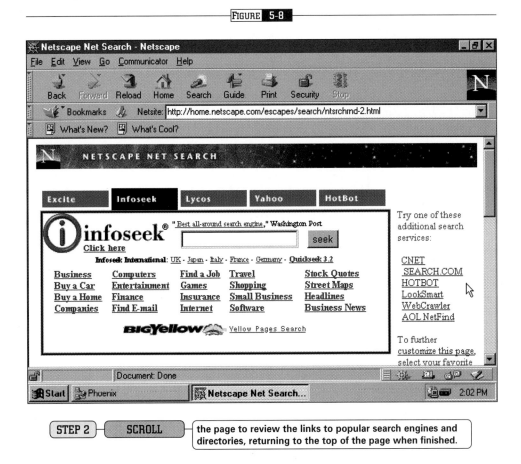

STEP 2 — SCROLL — the page to review the links to popular search engines and directories, returning to the top of the page when finished.

Search engines maintain indexes of key words used in Web pages. The indexes are updated automatically by software called *robots*. Robots follow links between pages throughout the entire WWW, adding any new Web pages to the search engines' indexes. You should use a search engine when you want to find a specific Web page. Some of the most popular search engines are AltaVista, Webcrawler, and CNET Search.com. To search for specific mailing list discussion groups, you can use a specialized search engine named Liszt. (You learned about mailing list discussion groups in Chapter 2.)

Directories use a subject-type format similar to that of a library card catalog. A directory provides a list of links to broad general categories of Web sites like Entertainment or Business Web sites. When you click one of those links, a subcategory list of links appears. For example, if you click the Entertainment link, you might see Movies, Television, and Video Games links. To find links to Web sites that contain information about movies, you would click the Movies link. Unlike a search engine, whose index is updated automatically, Web sites are added to directories only when an individual or a company asks that a particular Web site be included. Some directories also include review comments and ratings for the Web sites in their index. Most directories also provide an internal search engine (like the one you used on the Online or Offline Companion) that can be used only to search the directory's index, not the entire WWW. You use a directory when you are looking for information on broad general topics or if you are new to the WWW and want to discover the different kinds of information available. Popular directories include Yahoo! and Magellan Internet Guide.

The Web's many search tools are all constructed differently. That means you get varying results when you use several search engines or directories to search for information on the same topic. Do not assume that you know exactly how to use a particular search tool, because they all operate according to varying rules. For example, some search engines allow only a simple search on one keyword. Others allow you to refine your search by indicating that words placed in quotation marks must be found together, by indicating proper names, or by using special operators like "and," "or," and "not" to include or exclude search words. To save time, always begin by clicking the search tool's online Help link. Study the directions for using that particular search engine or directory, then proceed with your search.

5.h Using the Guide Feature to Find E-Mail Addresses and Company Information

When you need to search for e-mail addresses or find the address and phone number for anyone listed in telephone book white pages, you can use Navigator's Guide feature. Navigator's Guides provide quick access to Internet information, like e-mail directories. You can access the Guide feature by clicking the Guide button on the Navigation toolbar or by clicking the Guide subcommand under the Bookmarks command on the Communicator menu. To view the Guide menu:

STEP 1 — CLICK
the Guide button [Guide] on the Navigation toolbar

The Guide menu appears. Your screen should look similar to Figure 5-9.

FIGURE 5-9

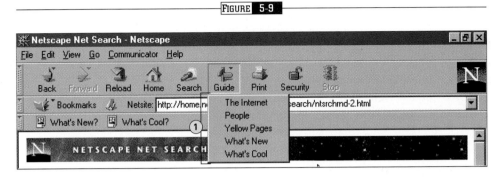

1. Guide menu

The Internet command loads a directory page with links to general areas of interest on the WWW like business, entertainment, or local news. You can use The Internet command to find Web sites classified in those general categories. You can use the People command to search a Web version of a phone book, with access to e-mail addresses instead of phone numbers. The People command also provides links to other "people-finder" Web pages, like Lycos PeopleFind. You can use the Yellow Pages command to search for business addresses and other business-related information.

Now that you are familiar with the possibilities offered by Navigator's Guide menu, you can close it. To close the Guide menu and reload your default home page:

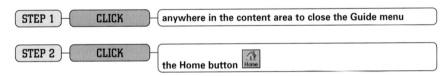

STEP 1 — CLICK — anywhere in the content area to close the Guide menu

STEP 2 — CLICK — the Home button

5.i Viewing Security Information

Information transmitted on Web pages may be secure (encrypted or scrambled), insecure (unencrypted), or mixed. A third party can read unencrypted files when they are being transmitted, so be sure you use only secure Web pages when you transmit sensitive information like credit card numbers.

When you want to know whether a Web page is secure or insecure, look at the Security indicator padlock icon on the status line. An unlocked padlock indicates an insecure Web page, while a locked padlock indicates a secure one.

To see more detailed information about the current page's security, click the Security indicator padlock icon or the Security button on the Navigation toolbar. To display the security information about the Netscape home page:

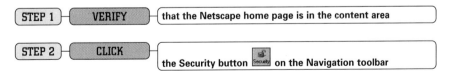

STEP 1 — VERIFY — that the Netscape home page is in the content area

STEP 2 — CLICK — the Security button on the Navigation toolbar

The Security Info window opens. Your screen should look similar to Figure 5-10.

FIGURE 5-10

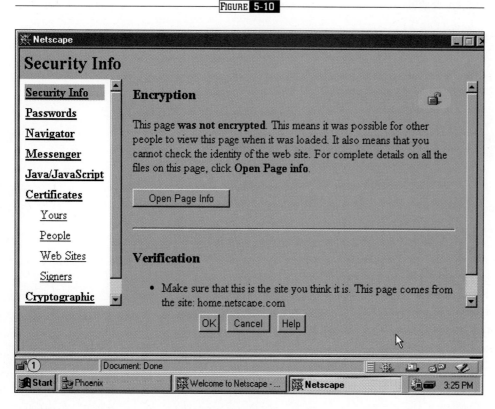

1. Security indicator

The Security Info window provides security details about the current page and links to additional security information. After you have read the details about the security of the current page, cancel the dialog box. To cancel the Security Info window:

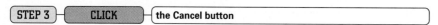

STEP 3 — CLICK — the Cancel button

For more information on levels of encryption, security indicators, and the various links in the Security Info window, see online Help. As an additional security measure, Navigator displays notification dialog boxes when you request a secure Web page or when you leave a secure Web page to display an insecure Web page. You see the notification dialog box only when you load a secure Web page.

You now are familiar with various Navigator toolbar buttons, shortcuts, and special features. In Chapter 6, you will use those features to browse the WWW. Close the Navigator application.

Summary

> Navigator provides many features and shortcuts to help you load Web pages.

> To load a Web page for the first time, you must know or find its URL. You often can find a URL by using a search engine or by finding print media that list the URL. You also can try to load the Web page by guessing the URL based on the company name and domain.

> You can enter a URL in the Open Page dialog box or type it directly in the Location box.

> After you load a Web page, you can save the Web page's URL as a bookmark. Later you can click the bookmark to load the Web page quickly.

> Bookmarks can be organized into folders in the Bookmarks window, much the same way you organize files in Windows Explorer.

> When pages are loaded, they are temporarily stored at your computer and are listed in a History list.

> You can use the Back and Forward buttons and commands to view pages from the History list.

> Previously loaded pages are listed at the bottom of the Go menu. You can view a previously loaded Web page by clicking the Web page on the Go menu or by selecting the Web page in the History window.

> You can set options and preferences about how Navigator looks and how some of its features work with the Edit, Preferences commands.

> Navigator's What's New, What's Cool, and Guide features provide links to new and interesting Web pages, pages that present information links by category, and e-mail and business directories.

> Navigator's Search page provides links to a variety of search engines and directories.

> The Security indicator on the status line tells you whether the current Web page is secure (encrypted) or insecure (unencrypted). The Security button on the Navigation toolbar displays more detailed information about the current page's security.

Commands Review

ACTION	MENU BAR	SHORTCUT MENU	MOUSE	KEYBOARD
Load a Web page using the Netsite or Location box			Select all or part of the current URL	Type the new URL in the Netsite or Location box
Add a new bookmark	Communicator, Bookmarks, Add Bookmark	Right-click a Web page in the content area, click Add Bookmark	Drag the Page Proxy icon to the Bookmarks button Bookmarks	ALT+C, B, K CTRL+D
Display the Bookmarks window	Communicator, Bookmarks, Edit Bookmarks		Click the Bookmarks button Bookmarks, click Edit Bookmarks	ALT+C, B, B CTRL+B
Display a Web page using a bookmark			Click the Bookmarks button Bookmarks, then click the bookmark	ALT+C, B, Down Arrow, Enter
Display a Web page using the Go menu	Go, then click the Web page in the list			ALT+G, then Down Arrow and ENTER; or press the key for the number to the left of the Web page title
Display a Web page using the History window	Communicator, History, then double-click an item in the History list			ALT+C, H
Review security on current Web page			Security	

Concepts Review

Circle the correct answer.

1. The Location box is sometimes called the:
[a] Bookmark QuickFile
[b] title bar
[c] Netsite box
[d] status line

2. The Security indicator is the:
[a] padlock icon.
[b] Page Proxy icon.
[c] Netscape icon.
[d] URL icon.

3. The content area contains the:
[a] Location box.
[b] Status line.
[c] History list.
[d] current Web page.

4. Bookmarks allows you to save:
[a] an HTML document into Navigator.
[b] the URL for a Web page you want to revisit.
[c] an HTML document to your hard disk.
[d] the keyword you use for a search.

5. To create a bookmark, you can use the:
[a] Page Proxy icon.
[b] Location box.
[c] Navigation toolbar.
[d] title bar.

6. Cache is a:
[a] temporary memory or hard-disk storage area.
[b] list of your bookmarks.
[c] security indicator.
[d] followed link.

SCANS

7. You cannot redisplay a previously loaded Web page by:
[a] clicking the Back or Forward command on the Go menu.
[b] clicking the Back or Forward button on the Navigation toolbar.
[c] dragging the Page Proxy icon to the status line.
[d] double-clicking an item in the History list.

8. You can change the way some Navigator features work by clicking the:
[a] Features command on the View menu.
[b] Preferences command on the Communicator menu.
[c] Preferences command on the Edit menu.
[d] Options command on the File menu.

9. Search engines update their indexes of keywords by software called:
[a] Webcrawler.
[b] Guides.
[c] Page Proxy.
[d] Robots.

10. Guides allow you to find:
[a] keywords for search engines.
[b] bookmarks.
[c] insecure Web sites.
[d] e-mail addresses.

Circle T if the statement is true or F if the statement is false.

1. T F The Bookmark QuickFile list contains a list of all the Web pages you have visited recently.
2. T F When you position the mouse pointer on a text or graphic link, the Location box displays the URL of that Web page.
3. T F The History list contains information about when and how many times a Web page was loaded.
4. T F When you first load a Web page, it is stored in your computer in the "Internet Storage Area."
5. T F The Personal toolbar allows you to create your own custom shortcuts to your favorite Web pages.
6. T F The Navigation, Location, and Personal toolbars can be hidden and unhidden with either menu commands or the mouse pointer.
7. T F To completely hide a toolbar and its tab, you must use the mouse pointer.
8. T F All search engines and directories maintain identical indices of Web pages.
9. T F A secure Web page is encrypted.
10. T F The Security Info window provides security details about the current page.

Fill in the blanks to complete the sentences.

1. The _____ toolbar is a customizable toolbar to which you can add bookmarks for files and Web pages.
2. Bookmarks are stored in _____.
3. When you load a Web page that hasn't changed since the last time you visited, the Web page loads from _____.
4. To hide a toolbar, click the _____.
5. AltaVista, Webcrawler, and CNET Search.com are some of the most popular _____.

6. Popular _____ include Yahoo and Magellan Internet Guide.

7. Directories use a(n) _____ format similar to the card catalog in a library.

8. Navigator's _____ provide quick access to Internet information such as e-mail directories.

9. A(n) _____ padlock indicates an insecure Web page.

10. A third party can read _____ files when they are transmitted.

Case Problems

PROBLEM 1: COMMUNICATE YOUR IDEAS

The employees in the sales department have recently started browsing the Web with Navigator and want to know how to create bookmarks and how to use the Personal toolbar. You have been asked to prepare a brief presentation on creating bookmarks and using the Personal toolbar. You will give your presentation at the next staff meeting.

Start Navigator. If you are using the Online Companion, load your school's home page or the Web page of your choice. To become more familiar with the Personal toolbar, display it and click each shortcut button in turn to review the Web page associated with the button. If your school has a Web page, load it and create a bookmark. (If your school does not have a home page, complete this problem with the Web page of your choice.) Drag the new bookmark you created to the Personal toolbar. Practice loading the Web page from the Personal toolbar. Delete the new bookmark from the Personal toolbar folder when you are finished.

If you are using the Offline Companion, load the Napier & Judd, Inc. Education Web page. Create a bookmark for the page. Drag the new bookmark you created to the Personal toolbar. Practice loading the Web page from the Personal toolbar. Delete the new bookmark from the Personal toolbar folder when you are finished.

Write an outline for your presentation that covers (1) creating bookmarks, and (2) how to add and remove bookmarks from the Personal toolbar.

PROBLEM 2: HELP

Your manager has created several HTML files with links to Web pages that he visits often. He asks you to find out if he can convert his "hotlists" to bookmarks so he can organize them efficiently in one bookmark file. You decide to search the Navigator's online Help system to see how to import HTML files as bookmarks.

Start Navigator, and use the online Help system to find the topic "To import HTML files (or hotlists) as bookmarks." Write down the steps for the process.

PROBLEM 3

Complete this problem using your ISP connection and the Internet.

You are working for a book publisher whose newest project is a series of books about popular movie actors and actresses from the 1920s to the 1950s, including Humphrey Bogart and Lionel Barrymore. The research director asks you to locate a list of movies that the actors starred in. You turn to Navigator and the WWW.

Connect to your ISP and open Navigator. Use the Search page to locate and link to the Yahoo directory home page. Click "Movies" in the Entertainment category, scroll down, click the Actors and Actresses link, and search for Humphrey Bogart. Link to the Web page that shows the filmography for Humphrey Bogart. Print the Web page that shows all the movies in which he appeared. Use the History list to return to the Actors and Actresses search page. Search for Lionel Barrymore, then link to and print the filmography for him. Close Navigator.

PROBLEM 4

Complete this problem using your ISP connection and the Internet.

You are the new secretary for the Business Women's Forum, a professional association. The president of the association has asked you to compile a list of Internet resources, which she will distribute at next month's lunch meeting.

Connect to your ISP, open Navigator, and use the Search page to locate and link to the AltaVista search engine home page. If you have not reviewed the AltaVista search engine online Help, do so now. Search for pages containing the keywords "women in business" (include the quotation marks). From the search results, click the URL or Web page title link of your choice to display the Web page. Review the new Web and its links. Create a bookmark to that page.

Use the Back button on the Navigation toolbar to redisplay the AltaVista home page, then click a different Web page title or URL link from the list. Review the Web page and its links. Create a bookmark for the Web page. Continue loading and reviewing pages until you have loaded and reviewed at least five pages.

Return to the default home Web page. Use the Go menu and the History list to reload at least three pages. Print two of the pages. Delete the bookmarks you added, then close Navigator.

Performing Common Business Tasks Using the WWW

" *The nature of my job is very fast-paced, and deadlines are always imminent. Integrating information from the Internet with Microsoft Office helps me do my job more efficiently. I can search the Web, lay out a publication, write a media release, and send an e-mail all within a short period of time.* "

Alison Steeves
community and public affairs officer

Sunnybrook Health Science Centre
Toronto, Canada

Sunnybrook Health Science Centre is one of the largest hospitals in Canada, housing the first and largest regional trauma unit in the country.

Chapter Overview:

In Chapter 5, you had a chance to practice using Navigator to load new Web pages and move back and forth through recently loaded Web pages. You also learned how to add bookmarks to the Bookmark QuickFile list and to the Personal Toolbar. In this chapter you will use those skills to search for travel-related information on the WWW.

SNAPSHOT

In this chapter you will learn to:

> Identify common business tasks

> Research flight schedules

> Make hotel reservations and rent a car

> Locate city maps

> Find entertainment activities and restaurants

> Locate other travel-related information

6.a Identifying Common Business Tasks

In the past, many everyday business tasks had to be accomplished using costly and time-consuming methods like sending paper correspondence or making lengthy telephone calls to vendors. Now you can save both time and money by using the Internet and the WWW. As described in Chapter 3, you can replace expensive paper correspondence with e-mail. In addition, you can contact vendors and find important information related to business using vendor Web sites. Before you attempt to use the WWW to handle business tasks, you should follow a few simple guidelines:

1. Make a list of the information you need.
2. Check your bookmarks to see if you already have shortcuts to the information you need.
3. Choose an appropriate search engine or directory to help you find information if you have not already created shortcuts.

Two common business tasks that are easy to accomplish using the WWW are making travel arrangements and locating travel-related information. In Chapter 3, you sent e-mail messages to the three branch managers in Toronto, Sydney, and London, asking them to confirm their attendance at the International Reinsurance Conference to be held in Boston next month. M. Barrett, the Toronto branch manager, asked you to make hotel and restaurant arrangements for him. Assume you also have received replies from B. Witherspoon in Sydney and C. Jones in London requesting flight schedule information, hotel reservations, car rental arrangements, and additional information about currency exchange rates, local weather, special events in Boston during the conference, and interesting restaurants in the city. You will use the WWW and the Online or Offline Companion to make the necessary travel arrangements and to locate the requested travel-related information for the branch managers.

Before you begin:

STEP 1 — START — the Navigator application

You can use the Online or Offline Companion for the activities in this chapter. If you are using the Offline Companion, go to the next series of steps. If you are using the Online Companion:

STEP 2 — TYPE — www2.coursetools.com/cti/AT/internet2/ in the Location: text box

STEP 3 — PRESS — the Enter key (↵ ENTER)

If you are using the Offline Companion:

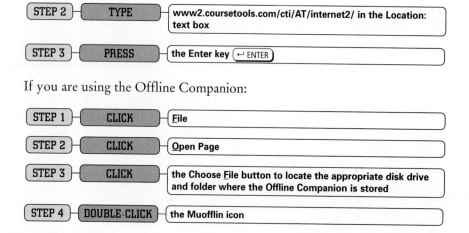

STEP 1 — CLICK — File

STEP 2 — CLICK — Open Page

STEP 3 — CLICK — the Choose File button to locate the appropriate disk drive and folder where the Offline Companion is stored

STEP 4 — DOUBLE-CLICK — the Muofflin icon

| STEP 5 | VERIFY | that the Navigator option button is selected |
| STEP 6 | CLICK | the Open button |

6.b Researching Flight Schedules

Instead of spending an hour or more on the phone with a travel agent, you can research flight schedules on your own using resources on the WWW. You can find Web pages for individual airlines as well as Web pages that provide links to multiple airlines. To locate flight schedule information:

| STEP 1 | CLICK | <u>Flight Schedules</u> link |

The flight schedules search results Web page appears and contains links to several individual airlines as well as a link to the Web page <u>Planes, Trains, Boats</u>, which summarizes links to multiple airlines. Your screen should look similar to Figure 6-1.

FIGURE 6-1

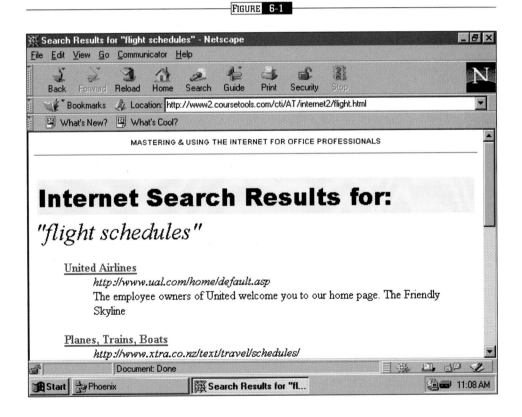

You need to find the schedule information on flights from London to Boston for C. Jones. Jones wants to leave London on the first of next month and return to London on the fifth. Because Jones is flying from London, you decide to check the flight schedules for British Airways. To locate flight schedule information for C. Jones:

| STEP 2 | CLICK | the <u>British Airways</u> link |

The British Airways home page loads. Your screen should look similar to Figure 6-2.

FIGURE 6-2

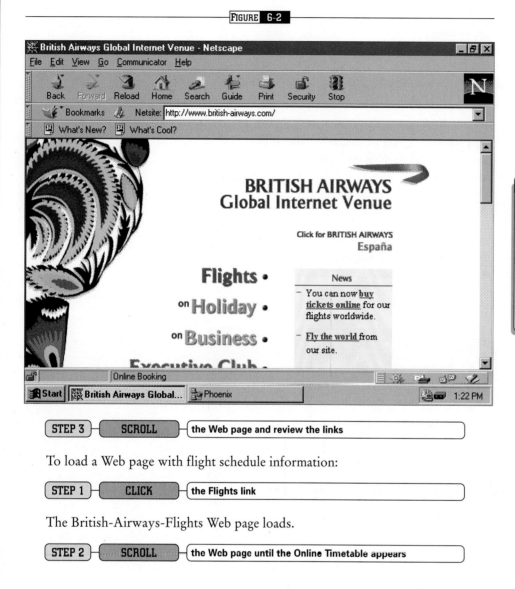

| STEP 3 | SCROLL | the Web page and review the links |

To load a Web page with flight schedule information:

| STEP 1 | CLICK | the Flights link |

The British-Airways-Flights Web page loads.

| STEP 2 | SCROLL | the Web page until the Online Timetable appears |

Except for the dates, your screen should look similar to Figure 6-3.

FIGURE 6-3

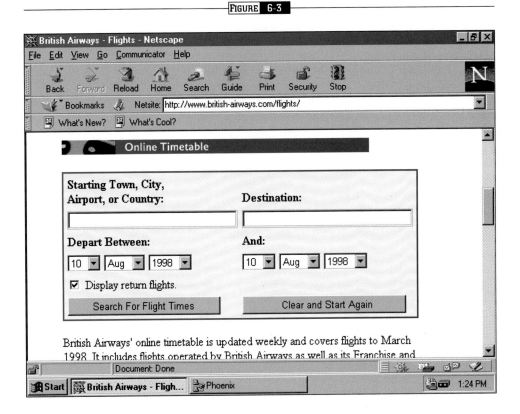

If you are using the Offline Companion, read but do not do the hands-on activities from this point to topic 6.c on page 101. Reload the Offline Companion.

To enter search criteria:

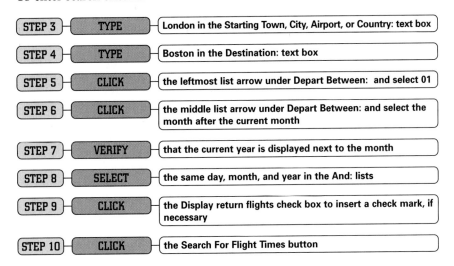

STEP 3	TYPE	London in the Starting Town, City, Airport, or Country: text box
STEP 4	TYPE	Boston in the Destination: text box
STEP 5	CLICK	the leftmost list arrow under Depart Between: and select 01
STEP 6	CLICK	the middle list arrow under Depart Between: and select the month after the current month
STEP 7	VERIFY	that the current year is displayed next to the month
STEP 8	SELECT	the same day, month, and year in the And: lists
STEP 9	CLICK	the Display return flights check box to insert a check mark, if necessary
STEP 10	CLICK	the Search For Flight Times button

A security information dialog box may appear advising you that any information you send is insecure (not encrypted). (You learned about Security indicators in Chapter 5.) Because the information about travel dates and locations you entered on this Web page is not particularly sensitive, you decide to continue the process. To continue:

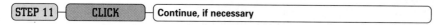

STEP 11 — CLICK — Continue, if necessary

In a few minutes, the Flights - Online Timetable Web page appears.

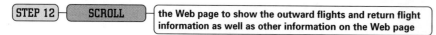

STEP 12 — SCROLL — the Web page to show the outward flights and return flight information as well as other information on the Web page

You now need to advise C. Jones of the possible flights. One way to do that is to copy the schedule information from the Web page to the Clipboard and then paste it into an e-mail message. Another way is to send the Web page uniform research locator (URL) as part of an e-mail message. The message's recipient can then click the URL to load the Web page. To create an e-mail message that includes the Flights - Online Timetable Web page URL:

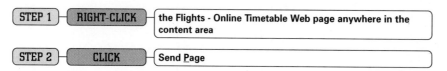

STEP 1 — RIGHT-CLICK — the Flights - Online Timetable Web page anywhere in the content area

STEP 2 — CLICK — Send Page

The Messenger Composition window opens with the insertion point in the To: text box, the Web page title in the Subject: text box, and the URL in your message area. Your screen should look similar to Figure 6-4.

FIGURE 6-4

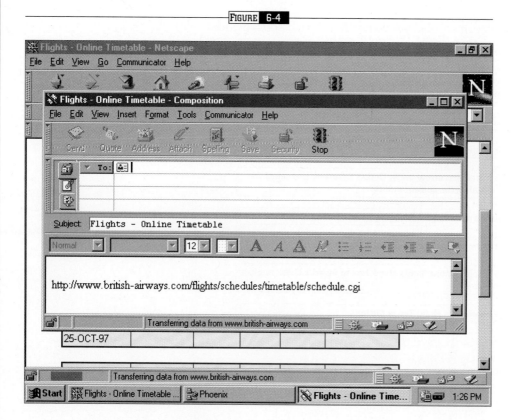

To complete and send the message:

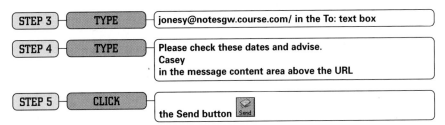

In a few seconds, the e-mail message is sent.

Now that you have found the flight information you need, you can take care of making hotel reservations and renting a car.

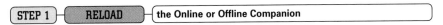

Once again, your starting point for this search is the Online or Offline Companion.

6.c Making Hotel Reservations and Renting a Car

Making hotel reservations and renting cars by phone can be a time-consuming process. Not only do you have to track down the correct phone numbers, you often have to wait on hold while the phone attendant deals with other callers. To speed up the process, many hotel and auto rental company now provide Web pages with links to data entry "forms" you can use to gather reservation data.

MAKING HOTEL RESERVATIONS

All three branch managers have asked you to reserve rooms at the Embassy Suites hotel. Using the WWW, you can locate the Embassy Suites hotel in the Boston area, review the room rates, and make a reservation for three rooms in your name. The managers plan to arrive after 5 p.m. on the first of next month and check out on the fifth. To find the Embassy Suites hotel Web page:

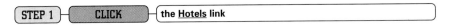

The "hotels and car rentals" search results page loads. To load the Embassy Suites home page:

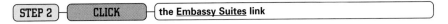

CAUTION

Do not send credit card information over the Internet unless you are using a secure Web site. Review the section on Security indicators in Chapter 5, if necessary.

The Embassy Suites home page loads. Your screen should look similar to Figure 6-5.

FIGURE 6-5

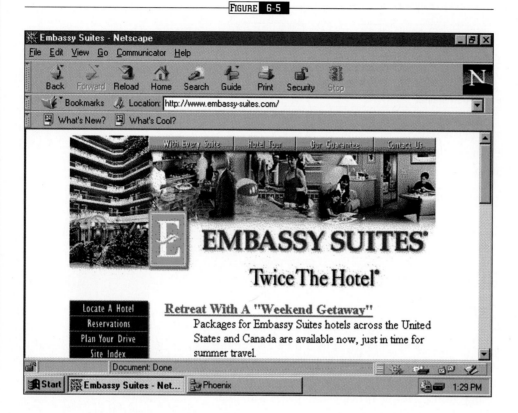

You will search the Embassy Suites Web site for a Boston-area hotel Web page. To search the Embassy Suites Web site:

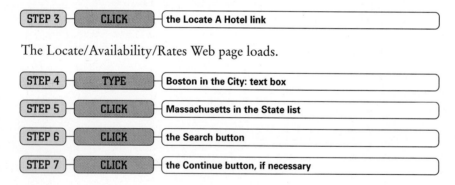

| STEP 3 | CLICK | the Locate A Hotel link |

The Locate/Availability/Rates Web page loads.

STEP 4	TYPE	Boston in the City: text box
STEP 5	CLICK	Massachusetts in the State list
STEP 6	CLICK	the Search button
STEP 7	CLICK	the Continue button, if necessary

The Embassy Suites, Boston-Marlborough, MA, Web page appears. Your screen should look similar to Figure 6-6.

FIGURE 6-6

1. Page Proxy icon

STEP 1 — SCROLL — the Web page and review the text and links

Because this is a Web page you can use the next time you want to access the Embassy Suites reservation information, you decide to create a bookmark for it.

STEP 2 — DRAG — the Page Proxy icon 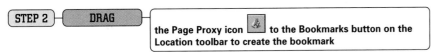 to the Bookmarks button on the Location toolbar to create the bookmark

Now you are ready to find information on room availability and rates. To check for availability and rates:

STEP 1 — CLICK — the Check Rates & Availability graphic link

If you are using the Offline Companion, read but do not perform Steps 2–5 on this page, or the steps on page 104. Begin the hands-on activities again at the top of page 105. The Check Availability Web page loads. To check room availability:

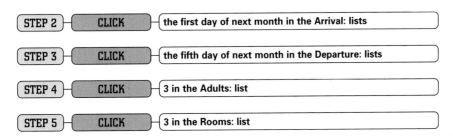

STEP 2 — CLICK — the first day of next month in the Arrival: lists

STEP 3 — CLICK — the fifth day of next month in the Departure: lists

STEP 4 — CLICK — 3 in the Adults: list

STEP 5 — CLICK — 3 in the Rooms: list

STEP 6	VERIFY	that Best Available Rate is selected in the Rate Category: list

STEP 7	CLICK	the Smoking: No option button

STEP 8	CLICK	the Check Availability button

STEP 9	CLICK	the Continue button, if necessary

The Make Reservations Web page loads.

STEP 1	SCROLL	the Web page to view the form and to make an online reservation

Each manager has requested a nonsmoking room with a king-size bed. The rooms should be billed to the main office, under your name. To enter the room selection and billing information:

STEP 1	CLICK	the KNG BASIC NONSMOKING option button

STEP 2	TYPE	Casey in the First name: text box

STEP 3	TYPE	Rivers in the Last name: text box

STEP 4	CLICK	the Address: Business option button

STEP 5	TYPE	1135 Newport Street in the Street: text box

STEP 6	TYPE	Boston in the City: text box

STEP 7	TYPE	MA in the State: text box

STEP 8	TYPE	02126 in the Zip: text box

STEP 9	CLICK	the Phone: Business option button

STEP 10	TYPE	617-556-3345 in the phone number text box

STEP 11	VERIFY	that American Express is selected in the Credit Card: list box

STEP 12	CLICK	September, 1999 in the Expiration Date: lists

STEP 13	TYPE	XXXXXXXXX in the Card Number: text box

STEP 14	CLICK	5 in the Est. Arrival: list

STEP 15	CLICK	the -PM option button, if necessary

If you were to continue by clicking the Make My Reservation button, the credit card information would be validated, and the reservations would be made. *Because you are using fictitious data, do not attempt to make the reservations.* Instead, return to the Online or Offline Companion to gather information on car rentals.

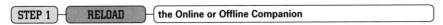

STEP 1 — **RELOAD** — the Online or Offline Companion

GETTING CAR RENTAL INFORMATION

Some car rental companies provide a Web page you can use to reserve a car, similar to the Web page you used to reserve the hotel rooms. Other companies provide only information and phone numbers to call for reservations. In addition, some car rental company home pages provide links to other related Web pages, like maps.

As the managers' travel date draws closer, you may have to arrange for cars for C. Jones and B. Witherspoon. You decide to review and compare the home pages for several auto rental companies now. That way, you will be prepared if you have to make car arrangements at the last minute. To display links to car rental Web pages:

STEP 1 — **CLICK** — the Car Rentals link

The "hotels and car rentals" search results page loads.

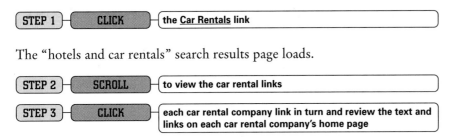

STEP 2 — **SCROLL** — to view the car rental links

STEP 3 — **CLICK** — each car rental company link in turn and review the text and links on each car rental company's home page

Next you turn your attention to finding the information the managers will need on their arrival in Boston.

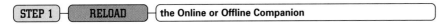

STEP 1 — **RELOAD** — the Online or Offline Companion

6.d Locating City Maps

You would like to have a city map available for each of the branch managers because they are not familiar with the Boston area. One way to find city maps is to use a link provided on a hotel or auto rental company Web page. However, those maps often are copyrighted, which means you cannot reproduce them. If you need to make copies of a map, you can search the WWW for maps in the public domain, that is, maps that are not copyrighted. A good place to look for public domain maps that you can print is a college or university online library. You will use the search engine in the Online or Offline Companion to locate and print a Boston city map. To search for city maps:

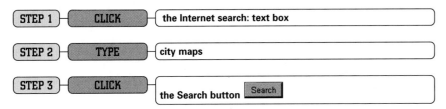

STEP 1 — **CLICK** — the Internet search: text box

STEP 2 — **TYPE** — city maps

STEP 3 — **CLICK** — the Search button `Search`

The "city maps" search results Web page loads. Notice that only one Web page in the Online or Offline Companion search engine index met the search criteria, the Web page for the Perry-Castañeda Library Map collection at the University of Texas at Austin.

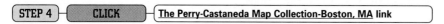

STEP 4 ⊢ CLICK ⊢ The Perry-Castaneda Map Collection-Boston, MA link

The Boston city map is a large graphic image that likely will take several minutes to load. When the Web page loads:

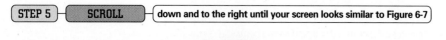

STEP 5 ⊢ SCROLL ⊢ down and to the right until your screen looks similar to Figure 6-7

─────────────── FIGURE 6-7 ───────────────

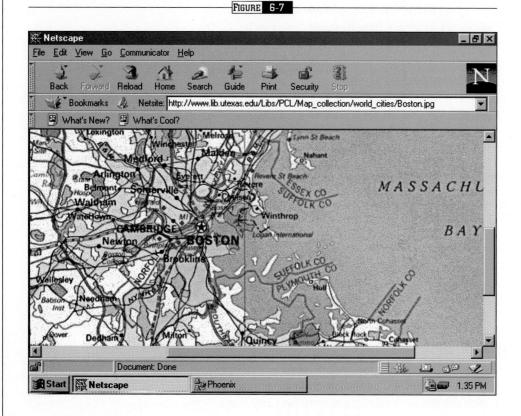

To print the map:

STEP 1 ⊢ CLICK ⊢ the Print button [Print] on the Navigation toolbar

The Print dialog box appears. To print 1 copy:

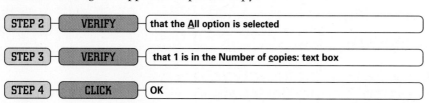

STEP 2 ⊢ VERIFY ⊢ that the All option is selected

STEP 3 ⊢ VERIFY ⊢ that 1 is in the Number of copies: text box

STEP 4 ⊢ CLICK ⊢ OK

One copy of the Boston city map is printed.

Your last task is to find some travel-related information about Boston. Once again, you begin your search from the Online or Offline Companion.

STEP 1 —| RELOAD |— the Online or Offline Companion

6.e Finding Entertainment Activities and Restaurants

The branch managers have requested your help in finding exciting restaurants and special entertainment events they can enjoy during their visit to Boston. You have been looking forward to browsing the WWW to locate information on entertainment activities and restaurants in the Boston area. This request gives you the opportunity to access several Boston Web pages, follow links to see where they lead, and find helpful and interesting information.

FINDING ENTERTAINMENT ACTIVITIES

To save time, think about a good starting point before you begin searching for information. Most major cities have Web pages with links to other Web pages that highlight city amenities and activities. Therefore, a good place to start to find information about a particular city is with that city's Web page. To display links to various cities Web pages:

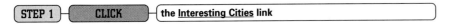
STEP 1 —| CLICK |— the Interesting Cities link

The "restaurants, entertainment, and special events" search results page loads. To load the Boston Web page:

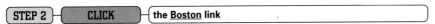
STEP 2 —| CLICK |— the Boston link

The Official City of Boston Web Site home page loads.

STEP 3 —| SCROLL |— the Web page and review the text and links

To display a current list of special events in the Boston area:

STEP 4 —| CLICK |— the City of Boston News and Events link at the very bottom of the page

A Web page loads that contains links to other pages with information about the Boston area.

If you are using the Offline Companion, read but do not perform the remaining steps 1–4.

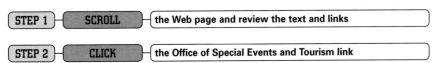
STEP 1 —| SCROLL |— the Web page and review the text and links

STEP 2 —| CLICK |— the Office of Special Events and Tourism link

A Web page loads that contains information about special events in the Boston area. Because a calendar or schedule of events can change, it would be a good idea to check this page frequently. To help you do that:

STEP 3 —| CREATE |— a bookmark on the Personal toolbar for the Boston-area special events page

QUICK TIP

Another way to load a city Web page is to go through Web sites maintained by third parties. For example, try the URL www.boston.com to load the Web site maintained by a Boston newspaper.

To continue:

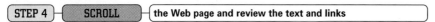

Now you need to find information about restaurants in the Boston area using the Online or Offline Companion.

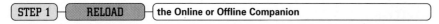

LOCATING INTERESTING RESTAURANTS

While reading the business section of your neighborhood newspaper, you saw an advertisement for a Web page that provides information on restaurants in the Boston area. You decide to search for similar Web pages with information about interesting restaurants the branch managers might enjoy.

If you are using the Offline Companion, read the rest of this section but do not attempt to perform the steps. You can begin performing the steps again in the next section, "Locating Other Travel-Related Information."

To find information on Boston restaurants:

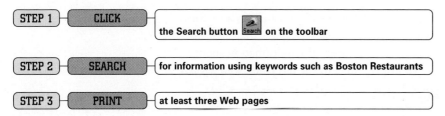

To finish the travel arrangements task, you need to find other travel-related information like currency exchange rates and the local weather forecast using the Online or Offline Companion.

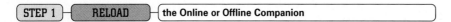

6.f Locating Other Travel-Related Information

Travelers usually have a host of questions about their destination. In the past, answering those questions entailed making numerous phone calls and consulting newspapers and books. Now you can find all the information you need on the WWW. Weather reports, currency exchange rates, and U.S. visa information are just a mouse click away.

GETTING WEATHER REPORTS

Many city home pages provide links to local weather and news. Also, some news and weather services maintain Web pages. You decide to use one of those services, Intellicast, to find the forecast for the Boston area. To find the forecast for the Boston area:

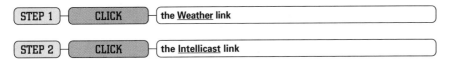

STEP 1 — CLICK — the **Weather** link

STEP 2 — CLICK — the **Intellicast** link

After a few moments, your screen should look similar to Figure 6-8.

FIGURE 6-8

1. Frame

Notice that a portion of the Intellicast Web page appears in its own window, with scroll bars. Such a scrollable window is called a **frame**. Frames allow Web page designers to present multiple Web pages on the same screen. A menu-type list of links appears down the left side of the framed Web page. You will scroll and review the page inside the frame and then link to a page with U.S.A. weather information link. To scroll the Web page inside the frame:

STEP 1 — SCROLL — the Web page vertically and horizontally and review the text and links

You want to view a Web page that contains weather information for the Boston area. To load a Web page containing weather information for the U.S.A.:

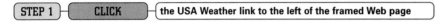

STEP 1 — CLICK — the USA Weather link to the left of the framed Web page

A page containing a U.S.A. weather map with major cities marked appears inside the frame. A new menu of links appears to the left of the framed page.

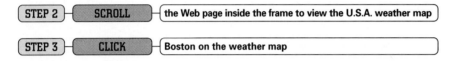

STEP 2 — SCROLL — the Web page inside the frame to view the U.S.A. weather map

STEP 3 — CLICK — Boston on the weather map

A page containing Boston's weather information now appears inside the frame and a new menu of links appears to the left of the framed page.

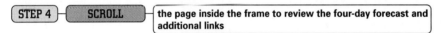

STEP 4 — SCROLL — the page inside the frame to review the four-day forecast and additional links

Next you return to the Online or Offline Companion to search for information useful to international travelers.

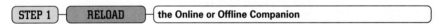

STEP 1 — RELOAD — the Online or Offline Companion

Finding Information for International Travel

Because your company has branch offices and clients around the world, you sometimes need to find international travel information such as foreign currency exchange rates, travel warnings, and other information provided by various embassies. To display a list of links to international travel information:

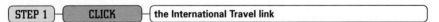

STEP 1 — CLICK — the International Travel link

The "international travel" search results page loads. Review the international travel links, delete any new bookmarks, and then close Navigator.

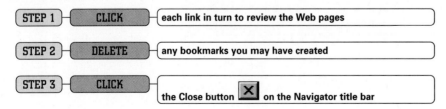

STEP 1 — CLICK — each link in turn to review the Web pages

STEP 2 — DELETE — any bookmarks you may have created

STEP 3 — CLICK — the Close button ☒ on the Navigator title bar

Summary

> You can save time and money using the Internet and the WWW to accomplish common business tasks.

> When you use the Web for business tasks, follow these guidelines: (1) make a list of the information you need; (2) check your bookmarks to see if you already have shortcuts to the information you need; and (3) choose an appropriate search engine or directory.

> You can use the WWW to make travel arrangements such as airline, hotel, and car rental reservations.

> Web sites often contain electronic forms you can use to send information (name, address, etc.) to vendors.

> You can send a Web page URL as part of e-mail message.

> You can find other travel information like area weather reports, currency exchange rates, city maps, and international travel information on the WWW.

> College or university online libraries often offer public domain maps you can print.

> Calendars of events on the WWW change often, so you should check them regularly.

> A frame is a scrollable window within a Web page.

Concepts Review

Circle the correct answer.

1. **Using the Internet and the WWW to find important information is:**
   [a] costly.
   [b] time consuming.
   [c] confusing.
   [d] time saving.

2. **Links on Web pages can be:**
   [a] text only.
   [b] graphics only.
   [c] text or graphics.
   [d] neither text nor graphics.

3. **A security information dialog box appears if you try to send information that is:**
   [a] secure.
   [b] insecure.
   [c] personal.
   [d] sensitive.

4. **To speed up the reservation process many hotel and auto rental companies now:**
   [a] provide Web pages with links to data entry forms.
   [b] hire more phone attendants.
   [c] accept reservations only by fax.
   [d] provide a private reservation number for Web page customers.

5. **A scrollable window within a Web page is called a:**
   [a] link.
   [b] page.
   [c] frame
   [d] bookmark.

6. **You can often find public domain maps that you can print from:**
   [a] car rental agencies.
   [b] hotels.
   [c] online encyclopedias.
   [d] college or university online libraries.

7. **Calendars of events on the Web usually change:**
   [a] often.
   [b] never.
   [c] weekly.
   [d] monthly.

8. **If you do not have a bookmark to an appropriate site to locate information, you should:**
   [a] look in the telephone directory.
   [b] use a search engine or directory.
   [c] call information.
   [d] send an e-mail.

9. **If you want someone else to look at a specific Web page, you should:**
   [a] call them and tell them the URL.
   [b] send them a letter with the URL.
   [c] send them an e-mail with the URL.
   [d] print the page and mail it to them.

Circle Ⓣ if the statement is true or Ⓕ if the statement is false.

1. Ⓣ Ⓕ You can save either time or money by using the Internet and the WWW to perform common business tasks.

2. Ⓣ Ⓕ Solving everyday business problems necessarily involves lengthy telephone calls.

3. Ⓣ Ⓕ If you do not already have a shortcut, you should use an appropriate search engine or directory to help you find information.

4. Ⓣ Ⓕ Individual airlines, hotels, and car rental agencies might have their own Web pages.

5. Ⓣ Ⓕ If a Web page takes a long time to load, you can click a text link without waiting for an accompanying picture to appear.

6. (T) (F) You can copy information from a Web page to the Clipboard and then paste it into an e-mail message.

7. (T) (F) It is safe to send credit card information over the Internet regardless of whether you are using a secure Web site.

8. (T) (F) You can reproduce any map you find on the Internet.

9. (T) (F) Frames allow Web page designers to add decorative borders to pages.

10. (T) (F) All browser programs can read and interpret Web pages with frames.

Fill in the blank to complete the sentence.

1. Only send credit card information over the Internet if you are using a(n) _____ site.

2. Before you reproduce a city map you find on the Web, you need to make sure it is in the _____.

3. A portion of a Web page that appears in its own window is called a(n) _____.

4. _____ allow Web page designers to present multiple Web pages on the same screen.

5. You can make such travel arrangements as airline, hotel, and car rental reservations using resources on the _____.

6. You can send a Web page URL as part of a(n) _____.

7. You can replace expensive paper correspondence with _____.

8. As a Web page loads, you can usually see the _____ links before any pictures.

9. If you send someone a Web site location in an e-mail, they can click the _____ to load the Web page.

Case Problems

PROBLEM 1

Complete this problem using the Online or Offline Companion.

You are executive secretary to Nora Lars, the sales manager for the international products division. Nora is leaving for an overseas trip to Sweden tomorrow and has asked you to find out the current exchange rate between U.S. dollars and Swedish krona.

   Start Navigator, load the Online or Offline Companion, and use the search engine to search for the keywords "international travel". Go to the World Currency Exchange site, and find out how much one dollar is worth in Swedish krona. Make sure the left frame uses US Dollars as the Base Currency and 1.00 as the Exchange Amount. Send the URL for the World Exchange Rates page to Nora Lars at the e-mail address: nora_lars@notesgw.course.com with the message "Here is the information you requested. Have a good and productive trip." Close Navigator when you are done.

PROBLEM 2: COMMUNICATE YOUR IDEAS

Complete this problem using the Online or Offline Companion.

You are secretary to the food distribution department in Food For All, an agency that's dedicated to eliminating world hunger. The coordinator is leaving for Cambodia next week and asks you to locate a Web site that she can access to find out the latest travel warnings for the region.

   Start Navigator, load the Online or Offline Companion, and use the search engine to search for the keywords "international travel". Go to the U.S. State Department Travel Warnings site. Link to the Travel Warnings & Consular Information Sheets page. Find out if Cambodia is on the list of current travel warnings. If it is, write a brief report summarizing the warning information. Close Navigator when you are finished.

PROBLEM 3

Complete this problem using the Online Companion.

You work for Conferences and More, a company that organizes conferences and trade shows. One of your responsibilities is to put together a packet to distribute to all attendees. Right now, you are working on a jewelry trade show that will take place in Atlanta in mid-January. The exhibitors and attendees will be coming from all over the world. You want to include the usual temperature ranges for the city during the trade show. You decide to include the weather for January and February because many international attendees are planning to extend their trips in order to tour the area.

Start Navigator, load the Online Companion and use the search engine to search for the keywords "weather." Go to the Intellicast site, load the page for USA Weather, and then find out the current weather forecast for Atlanta for the next four days. Then load the City Almanac and find the high and low temperatures in Atlanta during January and February. Print the City Almanac page for Atlanta. Close Navigator when you are finished.

PROBLEM 4

Complete this case problem using your ISP connection and the Internet.

You work for a not-for-profit fundraising company outside the city of San Francisco. To make the next event more unusual, the location manager wants to hold the event in a San Francisco museum. She asks you to track down a list of museums that are located within city limits.

Start Navigator and use an appropriate search engine to locate information about San Francisco museums. When you find a Web page that contains the information you need, print it. Write down the links you followed to get to this page. When you are finished, close Navigator.

SCANS

Commercial Activities on the WWW

Joseph Lee
president

Joseph Lee Design
North Kingstown, RI

Joseph Lee Design is a multidiscipline graphic design firm that specializes in creating books, CD-ROMs, Internet sites, and publications.

"

Being able to meet with our customers in person is not always possible; using the Internet allows us to give presentations remotely using our Web page. After seeing our designs, customers are able to give us immediate feedback using e-mail.

"

Chapter Overview:

In Chapter 6, you learned how to perform travel-related business tasks using the resources of the Web. In this chapter, you become acquainted with other commercial activities on the Web. First, you will learn how to use online banking, how to shop for products and services, and how to find vendor information and product support on the Web. Then you will research how to ship and track packages, find government information, find general business resources, search for potential employees, and post job openings.

SNAPSHOT

In this chapter you will learn to:

> Conduct banking transactions on the Web

> Shop for products and services on the Web

> Get vendor information on the Web

> Ship and track packages on the Web

> Find government information on the Web

> Find general business resources on the Web

> Conduct a job search and post jobs on the Web

7.a Conducting Banking Transactions on the Web

As manager of the Boston office, you are responsible for all the office's banking transactions. To avoid having to make weekly trips to the local bank, you want to begin managing the office checking accounts, savings accounts, and investments **online**, that is, over the Internet. Your company's vice president, J. Hillsdale, has asked you to research online banking services provided by banks in the area. You can use the Online or Offline Companion to research the banking options available on the Web.

Before you begin:

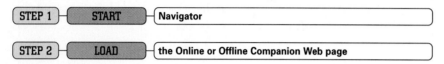

You will use the search engine to find a list of banks that offer online banking. To load a list of links to online banks:

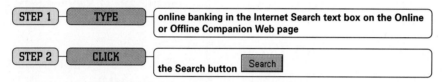

When the Search Results page for "online banking" loads:

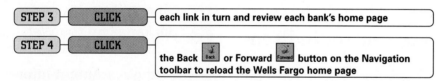

The Wells Fargo Bank provides a special demonstration of online banking. To take advantage of that feature, you will follow the links from the Wells Fargo home page to each of the online banking demonstration Web pages. Notice the Web page titles that appear on the Navigator title bar as you move from Web page to Web page. To follow the links from Web page to Web page and review the Wells Fargo demonstration:

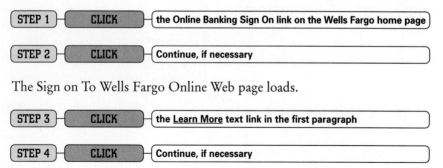

| STEP 1 | CLICK | the Online Banking Sign On link on the Wells Fargo home page |
| STEP 2 | CLICK | Continue, if necessary |

The Sign on To Wells Fargo Online Web page loads.

| STEP 3 | CLICK | the Learn More text link in the first paragraph |
| STEP 4 | CLICK | Continue, if necessary |

The Personal Banking Online Banking Web page loads. Your screen should look similar to Figure 7-1.

FIGURE 7-1

FIGURE 7-1

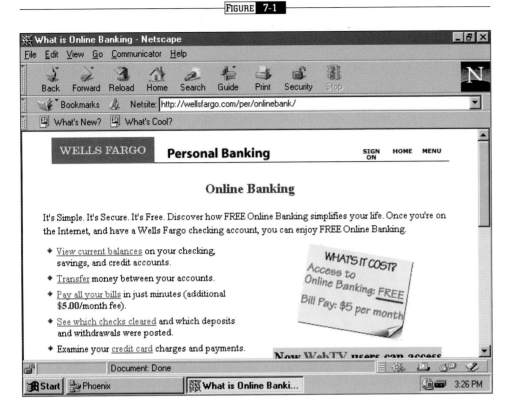

To start the online banking demonstration:

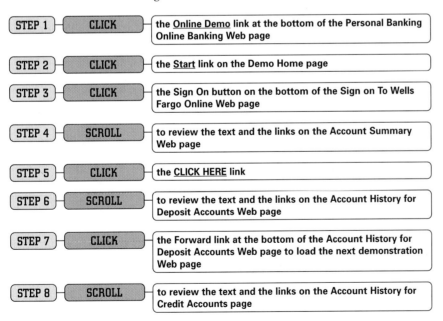

STEP 1	CLICK	the <u>Online Demo</u> link at the bottom of the Personal Banking Online Banking Web page
STEP 2	CLICK	the <u>Start</u> link on the Demo Home page
STEP 3	CLICK	the Sign On button on the bottom of the Sign on To Wells Fargo Online Web page
STEP 4	SCROLL	to review the text and the links on the Account Summary Web page
STEP 5	CLICK	the <u>CLICK HERE</u> link
STEP 6	SCROLL	to review the text and the links on the Account History for Deposit Accounts Web page
STEP 7	CLICK	the Forward link at the bottom of the Account History for Deposit Accounts Web page to load the next demonstration Web page
STEP 8	SCROLL	to review the text and the links on the Account History for Credit Accounts page

If you are using the Offline Companion, skip Steps 9 and 10.

| STEP 9 | CONTINUE | to load and review the remaining Wells Fargo banking demonstration Web pages by clicking the Forward link at the bottom of each page |

| STEP 10 | STOP | when you have completed the review and return to the Demo Home page |

When you have completed the review of the online banking demonstration, you should leave the Wells Fargo system and reload the Online or Offline Companion Web page.

| STEP 1 | RELOAD | the Online or Offline Companion Web page |

After reviewing the online banking options, you can now make a recommendation to J. Hillsdale about online banking for your company.

| STEP 1 | SEND | an e-mail message to J. Hillsdale briefly discussing the online banking options available and making your recommendation. J. Hillsdale's e-mail address is jhillsdale@notesgw.course.com |

Another type of commercial transaction on the Web that is becoming more popular is shopping for products or services. In the next section, you will use the Online or Offline Companion to discover how to shop for and purchase items online.

7.b Shopping for Products and Services on the Web

As the office manager, you frequently purchase items for your company, such as office supplies, postage, and flowers for clients. You also purchase all office systems software and computer-related products.

Many vendors maintain pages on the Web to provide product information and customer service. Such pages often supply phone numbers and e-mail addresses you can use to place orders or online order forms similar to the hotel reservation form you used in Chapter 6. You also can find Web pages that are like online "shopping malls," providing links to a variety of different companies' products and services.

Paying for Online Internet Purchases

You can pay for online purchases by using a secured (encrypted) credit card transaction, a secured (encrypted) electronic checking account transaction, a company that can approve and collect for your purchase, or "electronic cash," sometimes called **ecash** or **cyber money**.

You should use a credit card to pay for online purchases only via secure (encrypted) Web pages. A secure Web page provides about the same level of security as giving your card number to someone over the telephone or presenting your card to a cashier in a store. (You used a credit card in this manner to secure a hotel reservations in Chapter 6.)

To learn more about using a third-party approval/collection service and electronic cash, you can use the search engine on the Online or Offline Companion. To search for Web pages with information about electronic cash:

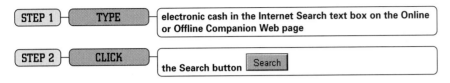

STEP 1 — TYPE — electronic cash in the Internet Search text box on the Online or Offline Companion Web page

STEP 2 — CLICK — the Search button [Search]

The Search Results page for "electronic cash" loads.

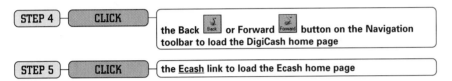

STEP 3 — CLICK — each link in turn to review the home pages presented in the Search Results page

Suppose you want to know more about the DigiCash electronic cash options:

STEP 4 — CLICK — the Back [Back] or Forward [Forward] button on the Navigation toolbar to load the DigiCash home page

STEP 5 — CLICK — the Ecash link to load the Ecash home page

It may take several minutes to load the Ecash page. After the page loads, your screen should look similar to Figure 7-2.

FIGURE 7-2

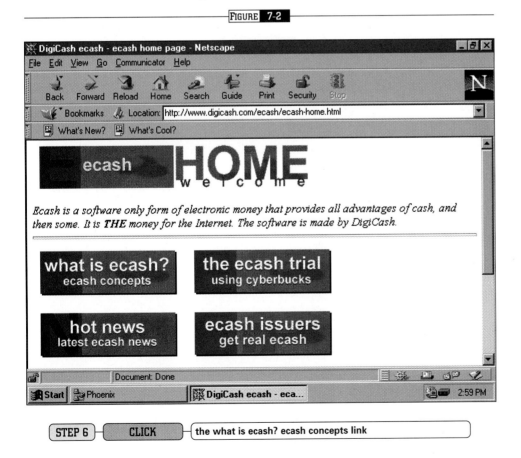

STEP 6 — CLICK — the what is ecash? ecash concepts link

The Digicash ecash - about ecash Web page loads. Your screen should look similar to Figure 7-3.

FIGURE 7-3

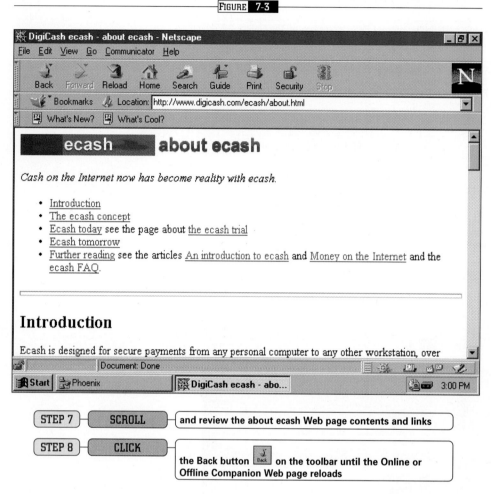

STEP 7 — SCROLL and review the about ecash Web page contents and links

STEP 8 — CLICK the Back button 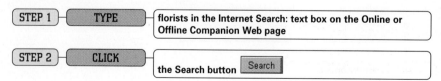 on the toolbar until the Online or Offline Companion Web page reloads

Now that you're familiar with ecash, you can explore some of the products you can purchase with it. In the next section, you'll learn how to purchase items over the Web.

PURCHASING ITEMS ONLINE

A quick way to find companies that sell their products and services online is to search for a particular company or product and then load the desired home page. You also can load an **online shopping mall,** which is a Web page with links to a variety of companies and services. For example, suppose you need to send flowers to a client in Australia. You can use the Internet to locate florists for local, national, and international deliveries and then order the flowers online. To use the search engine in the Online or Offline Companion to search for florists:

STEP 1 — TYPE florists in the Internet Search: text box on the Online or Offline Companion Web page

STEP 2 — CLICK the Search button | Search |

The Search Results page for "florists" loads.

| STEP 3 | CLICK | each link in turn to review the home pages in the list |

Because your order is for an international delivery, you decide to use the FTD International Catalog link.

| STEP 4 | CLICK | the Back 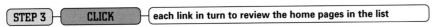 or Forward button to reload the FTD International Catalog Web page |

STEP 5	SCROLL	the Web page and review the contents and links
STEP 6	CLICK	the Pull Down to Select list arrow
STEP 7	CLICK	Australia
STEP 8	CLICK	the Go link
STEP 9	CLICK	Continue, if necessary

Your screen should look similar to Figure 7-4.

FIGURE 7-4

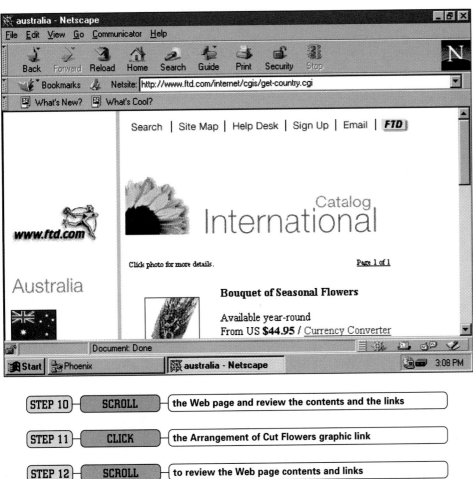

STEP 10	SCROLL	the Web page and review the contents and the links
STEP 11	CLICK	the Arrangement of Cut Flowers graphic link
STEP 12	SCROLL	to review the Web page contents and links

At this point, you could order the bouquet and pay for it with ecash (if you have an ecash account) or with a credit card. Or you could reload the previous Web page and review different arrangements before making your selection. Because you are only practicing, stop and return to the Online or Offline Companion. *Do not attempt to order any flowers.*

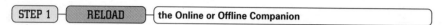

STEP 1 — RELOAD — the Online or Offline Companion

More and more companies are finding ways to use the Web to sell their products. In the next section, you will learn how to use the Online or Offline Companion to locate information on vendors who sell products commonly used in business.

7.c Getting Vendor Information on the Web

Many companies support pages on the Web to advertise their products and services. They also provide information for people interested in investing in their company. You can use those Web pages to get information about new products that might be useful for your business.

For example, suppose you need to replenish the office postage supply. J. Hillsdale suggests using a postal service called E-Stamp to purchase postage stamp supplies online. To locate the E-Stamp Web page:

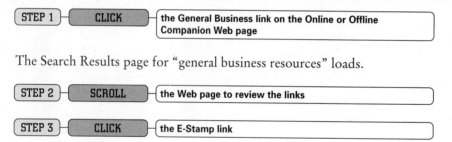

STEP 1 — CLICK — the General Business link on the Online or Offline Companion Web page

The Search Results page for "general business resources" loads.

STEP 2 — SCROLL — the Web page to review the links

STEP 3 — CLICK — the E-Stamp link

The E-Stamp Web page loads. Your screen should look similar to Figure 7-5.

FIGURE 7-5

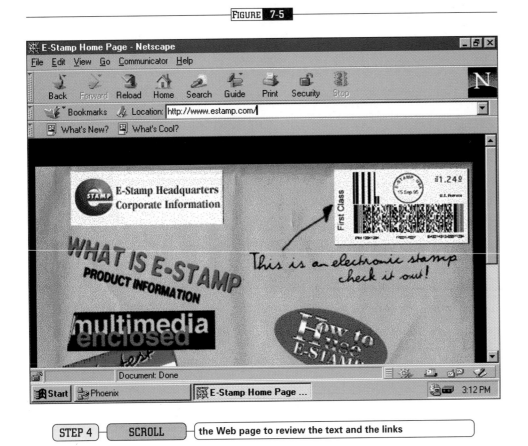

STEP 4 — SCROLL — the Web page to review the text and the links

To inform J. Hillsdale about the E-Stamp company, you decide to send the Web page as an e-mail, a technique you learned in Chapter 6. To send the E-Stamp page as e-mail:

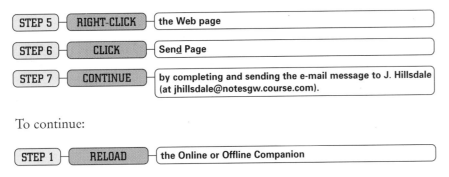

STEP 5 — RIGHT-CLICK — the Web page

STEP 6 — CLICK — Send Page

STEP 7 — CONTINUE — by completing and sending the e-mail message to J. Hillsdale (at jhillsdale@notesgw.course.com).

To continue:

STEP 1 — RELOAD — the Online or Offline Companion

Now, suppose you want to purchase the most recent version of a computer software application, like Communicator, or get information about trends in a specific industry, or get customer service a particular product you are already using. You can use a search engine to search for Web pages that provide company and product information, or you can use the Online or Offline Companion to load links to Web pages that provide product and customer support.

To load links to a variety of company Web pages that provide company information and product support:

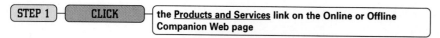

The Search Results page for "general business resources" loads. As you can see from the list of links, most major companies now provide Web sites to make it easier for their customers and potential customers to get information.

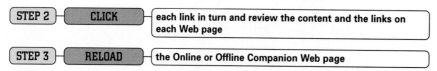

7.d Shipping and Tracking Packages on the Web

One of the many important business-related tasks you can perform on the Web is the shipping and tracking of packages. In this section, you will use the Online or Offline Companion to find shipping services available on the Web.

The staff in the Boston office often must send packages to the London and Sydney branch offices as well as to clients around the world. As the office manager, you must be able to send and track important packages easily, regardless of their destinations. J. Hillsdale has asked you to research how to use the Web to arrange for shipping and tracking packages. Once again, you will use the search engine to display a list of links to Web pages containing the information you want. To display a list of shipping company links:

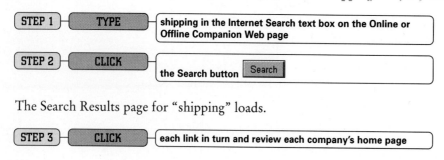

The Search Results page for "shipping" loads.

STEP 3 — CLICK — each link in turn and review each company's home page

Suppose you want to know more about the online services offered by Federal Express. After you find the information, you need to inform J. Hillsdale of the available options. You decide to send the URL of the Federal Express home page in an e-mail message. To find Federal Express's online service options:

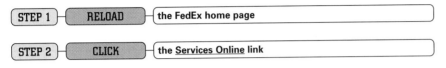

| STEP 1 | RELOAD | the FedEx home page |
| STEP 2 | CLICK | the Services Online link |

Your screen should look similar to Figure 7-6.

FIGURE 7-6

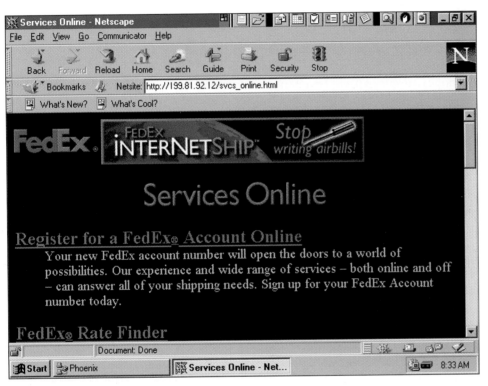

| STEP 3 | SCROLL | the Services Online Web page and review the contents and the links |

To attach the Services Online home page to an e-mail message to J. Hillsdale:

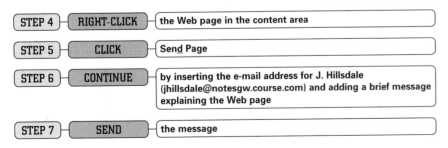

STEP 4	RIGHT-CLICK	the Web page in the content area
STEP 5	CLICK	Send Page
STEP 6	CONTINUE	by inserting the e-mail address for J. Hillsdale (jhillsdale@notesgw.course.com) and adding a brief message explaining the Web page
STEP 7	SEND	the message

In the next section, you will use the Online or Offline Companion to find information about government services on the Web.

STEP 1 ┤ RELOAD ├ the Online or Offline Companion

7.e Finding Government Information on the Web

As the office manager, you sometimes are required to get information from the Commonwealth of Massachusetts, U.S. federal, Ontario province, and Canadian national government offices. Getting the information used to involve long phone calls and occasional trips to the public library. Even then, you could never be absolutely certain that the information you'd acquired was official and up-to-date. You've decided to search for information on the Web, because you know that a government Web page is a quick and reliable source of information. To display a list of government Web pages:

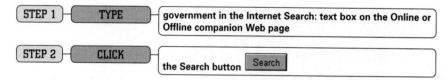

STEP 1 ┤ TYPE ├ government in the Internet Search: text box on the Online or Offline companion Web page

STEP 2 ┤ CLICK ├ the Search button Search

The Search Results page for "government" loads. Notice that the list includes state, federal, and foreign government Web pages.

STEP 3 ┤ CLICK ├ each link in turn and review the contents and the links on the Web pages in the list

Each government Web site provides a different type and level of information. For example, the Commonwealth of Massachusetts Web site provides links to different state agencies, while the Internal Revenue Service Web site is an online magazine updated daily with news about changes to tax laws, links to new tax forms, and special taxpayer information. You can use the information provided at government Web sites to get the most up-to-date instructions, forms, and regulations that affect your business.

You also can locate good general business information when you are browsing the Web by following links from page to page. In the next section, you will use the Online or Offline Companion as a starting point to finding general business information.

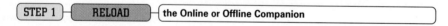

STEP 1 ┤ RELOAD ├ the Online or Offline Companion

QUICK TIP

You can right-click the content area of a Web page and then click the Back or Forward command to navigate between recently loaded Web pages.

7.f Finding General Business Resources

The Web contains helpful general information for businesses and professional associations. You can find summary pages with multiple links to other business pages, information of interest to professional accountants, world and financial news, stock quotes, and much more. You can use the Online or Offline Companion to display a sample of general business and professional interest Web pages. To display a list of Web pages containing general business and professional information:

STEP 1 — **CLICK** — the <u>General Business</u> link on the Online or Offline Companion Web page

The Search Results page for "general business resources" loads. The links on this page provide a sample of the different types of general business resources available on the Web.

STEP 2 — **CLICK** — each link in turn and review the contents and the links on each Web page

After you finish reviewing the general business resources links, you will take a look at another way to use the Web that is becoming increasingly important to both companies and individuals. Companies looking for employees and individuals searching for jobs are now turning to the Web to meet those needs. The Online or Offline Companion provides links to Web sites devoted to job search.

STEP 1 — **RELOAD** — the Online or Offline Companion Web page

7.g Conducting a Job Search and Posting Jobs on the Web

If you are looking for employment or for an employee, the Web is the place to begin your search. In fact, performing job searches is one of the most popular uses of the Web. If you want to work for a particular company, try going to that company's home page and looking for a link to a page of job openings. As you might expect, some Web sites are devoted exclusively to the job search process. Such Web sites include pages with links to job postings, resume writing tips, space to post a resume, and hiring companies' URLs and e-mail addresses. If you are looking for a job, consider posting your resume at one of those Web sites. Also, many online magazines and newspapers maintain "classified" Web pages with job postings.

Suppose you want to hire someone to provide computer software and systems support for the Boston and Toronto branch offices of WorldWide Insurance Brokers, Inc. You can use the Online or Offline Companion to search for resumes on potential employees and to post your company's open positions for review by job seekers. To find Web pages with employment information:

STEP 1 — **CLICK** — the <u>Employment</u> link on the Online or Offline Companion Web page

The Search Results page for "employment links" loads.

STEP 2 — CLICK — each link in turn to review the contents and the links on each Web page

Suppose you want to know more about how to post your company's job opening on the Web.

STEP 3 — RELOAD — the JobWeb Resources home page

Your screen should look similar to Figure 7-7.

FIGURE 7-7

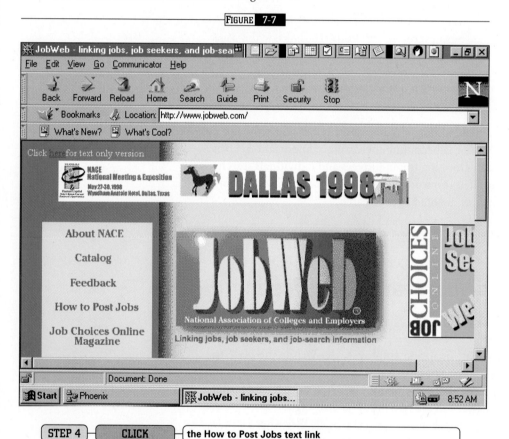

STEP 4 — CLICK — the How to Post Jobs text link

This Web page provides additional information about JobWeb's services and for customers to register, or subscribe, to those services. While much of the information on the Web is free, some Web sites, like this one, require you to subscribe and sometimes pay a fee before you can access their services. *Do not register or subscribe to JobWeb now.* You will follow links on this page to learn more about JobWeb and print a Web page that gives information on costs and services.

STEP 5 — CLICK — the <u>Learn more</u> text link

STEP 6 — SCROLL — to review the Web page contents and links

STEP 7 — CLICK — the Print button 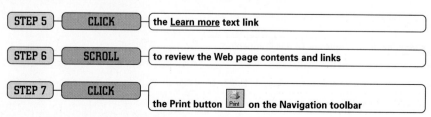 on the Navigation toolbar

The JobWeb site is a large one with many linked pages. Some very large Web sites provide a "picture" of all the links at the site on one page. That picture, which can consist of graphic or text links, is called a **site map**. Site maps help you quickly find a link to a specific page at a Web site. To load and view the JobWeb Resources site map Web page:

STEP 1 — CLICK — the Map of Job Web Resources link at the top of the Web page

Your screen should look similar to Figure 7-8.

FIGURE 7-8

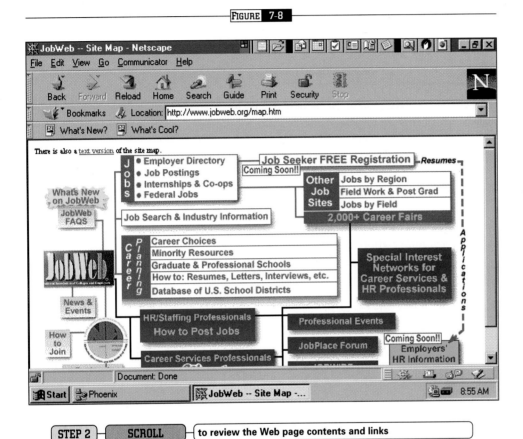

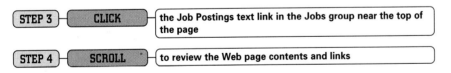
STEP 2 — SCROLL — to review the Web page contents and links

Next, you decide to review current job postings so you can get some ideas on how to format the WorldWide Insurance Brokers job posting. To review current job postings:

STEP 3 — CLICK — the Job Postings text link in the Jobs group near the top of the page

STEP 4 — SCROLL — to review the Web page contents and links

If you are using the Offline Companion, read Steps 5–10, but do not do them.

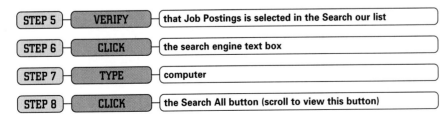
STEP 5 — VERIFY — that Job Postings is selected in the Search our list

STEP 6 — CLICK — the search engine text box

STEP 7 — TYPE — computer

STEP 8 — CLICK — the Search All button (scroll to view this button)

A Web page with a list of computer-related job postings loads. The list is updated on a daily basis, so it is a good idea to check the list (and any similar lists you find) regularly when you are looking for a job. Don't forget to check the home page for any company that posts jobs in a list like this one. It is likely that the company home page will contain additional links to pages with employment opportunities at the company.

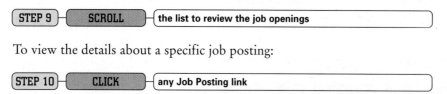

STEP 9 — SCROLL — the list to review the job openings

To view the details about a specific job posting:

STEP 10 — CLICK — any Job Posting link

A Web page with the details about the job position loads. Notice that from this Web page you can get specific information about the job posting, such as the job description, educational requirements, work experience requirements, and benefits. Additionally, many of the job-detail Web pages also provide excellent information about the company that is posting the job. The information provided on the detailed job-posting Web page can also provide a format for you to use to post jobs for World-Wide Insurance Brokers, Inc. *Do not post a job to JobWeb at this time.*

You are now familiar with the kinds of commercial activities that take place on the Web. You reviewed Web sites that offer online banking, product support, and services that you can purchase with electronic cash or by credit card. Additionally, you researched how to locate government and general business information on the Web. In the next chapter, you will learn how to create your own company Web site so that WorldWide Insurance Brokers, Inc can promote their services to potential clients around the world.

STEP 1 — CLOSE — Navigator

Summary

> You can manage a variety of accounts and investments securely with an online banking Web page.

> You can pay for goods and services online by using secured credit card transactions, a company that approves and collects for purchases, or electronic cash (ecash).

> Vendor information and product or customer support are readily available on vendor Web sites.

> You can ship and track packages by using a shipping company's Web page.

> Many local, state, federal, and foreign governments maintain pages on the Web.

> The Web contains many pages of good general information for businesses and professional associations.

> You can use the Web to search for job openings, post your resume, or post job openings for your company.

Concepts Review

Circle the correct answer.

1. If you manage your checking accounts online, you are processing information by:
[a] Internet.
[b] telephone.
[c] person.
[d] e-mail.

2. You cannot pay for an online purchase with:
[a] a secured online credit card.
[b] electronic cash.
[c] a third-party approval/collection company.
[d] cash.

3. An online shopping mall is a Web page from which you can:
[a] find information about only one company's products.
[b] order only flowers.
[c] borrow cyber money.
[d] find links to a variety of companies and services.

4. Ecash is an abbreviation for:
[a] encrypted money.
[b] e-mail money.
[c] electronic money.
[d] electronic checking.

5. A government Web page is:
[a] rarely accurate.
[b] usually out-of-date.
[c] often quick and reliable.
[d] less official than what you can find in the library.

6. To move between recently loaded Web pages, you can:
[a] right-click the content area and then click Back or Forward.
[b] right-click the Navigation toolbar and then click Forward.
[c] click the content area.
[d] double-click the content area.

7. A Web page that contains a "picture" of all the links at a Web site is called a:
[a] content area.
[b] site map.
[c] document map.
[d] link area.

8. Giving your credit card number to someone over the telephone provides the same level of security as sending credit card information over:
[a] a secure Web page.
[b] an insecure Web page.
[c] an unencrypted Web page.
[d] an unscrambled Web page.

9. The E-Stamp Web page:
[a] provides credit checks.
[b] sells rubber stamps.
[c] collects e-cash from past-due accounts.
[d] sells postage stamp supplies.

Circle T if the statement is true or F if the statement is false.

1. T F A quick way to find companies that sell their products and services online is to use a search engine.

2. T F You should always use an insecure order document or form when paying for online purchases by credit card.

3. T F A third-party approval/collection service provides "electronic cash" for online purchases.

4. T F All vendors allow you to order directly from their home pages.

5. T F You can purchase the latest version of some companies' computer software online.

6. T F Using a credit card to pay for online purchases is too risky and should be avoided at all costs.

7. T F You can ship and track packages from a shipping company's Web page.

8. T F You can use the WWW to search for or post job openings.

9. T F Ecash is different from cyber money.

10. T F A site map shows links to only one Web page.

Fill in the blank to complete the sentence.

1. To avoid weekly trips to the local bank, you can manage your checking account and investments _____.

2. Electronic money is sometimes called ecash or _____.

3. A(n) _____ is a Web page with links to a variety of companies and services.

4. You can purchase postage stamp supplies online from the _____ Web page.

5. To navigate between recently loaded Web pages, right-click the _____ of the Web page and click the appropriate command.

6. Many Web pages provide phone numbers, e-mail addresses, or online _____ that you can use to place orders for products.

7. A(n) _____ is an area on a Web page that contains multiple links to other pages at a Web site.

8. A site map link can be either _____ or text links.

9. A(n) _____ Web page provides the same level of security as giving your credit card to a cashier in a store.

Case Problems

PROBLEM 1

Complete this problem using your ISP connection and the Internet.

You are the administrative assistant to the president of Outdooraganza, a store that specializes in camping equipment and heavy-duty outdoor clothing. The president wants to begin advertising the company's products on the Internet. It's your job to locate several online shopping malls that you think would be appropriate to advertise on, and to print copies of each.

Start Navigator and use the search engine of your choice to search for "online shopping malls." Review the list of Web pages. Load the home pages for at least three online malls that use secure Web pages and that you think would be an appropriate place for Outdooraganza to advertise; set a bookmark for each. Use the bookmarks to return to each page and then print it. Delete the bookmarks and then close Navigator.

PROBLEM 2: COMMUNICATE YOUR IDEAS

Complete this problem using your ISP connection and the Internet.

As the local office manager for a nationwide real estate company, you are responsible for purchasing supplies and products for your office. You notice that you are running low on some items and decide to look for companies that sell office products on the Internet. As a good comparison shopper, you want to get three price estimates for each of the following items: 1 box (100 folders) of manila file folders and 1 case (10 reams, 500 sheets per ream) of 8½"-by-11" 20-lb. white copier paper.

Start Navigator and use search engines or other Netscape features to find companies that sell office supplies and products online. Find the price for each of the two items listed above at three different online stores. Print the pages that show the prices for the items. Close Navigator and then write a report that answers the following questions: Are the prices for each item the same at all stores? From which company or companies would you purchase the items? Why? Is the site you chose a secure site for sending credit card information?

PROBLEM 3

Complete this problem using the Online Companion.

You are the administrative assistant at a mail-order coffee company. The executive board has decided they want to expand operations and start selling coffee over the Internet. They have researched the various online malls and advertising possibilities but want to know more about payment options over the Internet. They ask you to locate that information.

Start Navigator, load the Online Companion, and search for "electronic cash." Load the DigiCash home page, load the Ecash home page, click the what is ecash? link, scroll to the Further Reading section, then click the Money on the Internet link. Read about the different methods to pay for purchases online. In two or three paragraphs, discuss and compare the different payment methods. Which method would you feel most comfortable using? Explain why. When you are finished, close Navigator.

PROBLEM 4: HELP

Complete this problem using the Online or Offline Companion.

You work for a management consulting firm that finds unique solutions to business problems. Many of the firm's clients are asking whether the Internet and the World Wide Web are secure places on which to conduct business. You decide to find out more on that subject from Navigator's online Help system.

Start Navigator and load the Online or Offline Companion. Click the Security button on the Navigation toolbar. Read the information that appears. Click the Help button. Find the section About Security and learn how to make it more difficult for unauthorized users to access your system and correspondences. Write down the seven things you can do to make your system more secure. Read further to define any terms that are unfamiliar to you. When you are finished, close Navigator.

Establishing a Presence on the Web

> *Being able to access information quickly and accurately is critical to the success of any business. Using the Web as a resource allows our employees to get the most accurate and up-to-date information immediately.*

Myrna D'Addario
senior vice president, technology

*Course Technology
Cambridge, MA*

Course Technology is a leading publisher of technology-based educational materials.

Chapter Overview:

The commercial Web pages you downloaded in Chapter 7 are only a sample of the thousands of Web pages maintained by companies on the Web. Businesses of every kind use their Web sites to advertise and sell their goods and services to the millions of potential customers browsing the Web each day. WorldWide Insurance Brokers, Inc wants to establish a Web site to promote its insurance brokerage services to potential clients around the world. In this chapter you will learn how to plan, design, and create a simple Web site for WorldWide Insurance Brokers, Inc.

SNAPSHOT

In this chapter you will learn to:

> **Set goals and objectives for your Web site**

> **Define the structure of your Web site**

> **Design an effective Web page**

> **Use HTML to create Web pages**

> **Use Composer to create Web pages**

> **Test your Web pages**

> **Publish your Web pages**

> **Get your Web site noticed**

8.a Setting Goals and Objectives for Your Web Site

Creating an effective Web site begins with determining the goals for the Web site. Along with advertising and selling goods and services, Web sites also can be used to gather data about prospective customers, provide customer support online, build a positive image of a company, and entertain potential customers.

To help you determine the goals for your Web site, begin by asking if you want your Web site to:

- advertise products and services?
- allow customers to order products and services online?
- provide customers online product support?
- build a corporate image?
- collect information about current and potential customers?
- provide links to related Web pages?
- provide general or industry information?

Your answers to those questions will help you determine the overall purpose of your Web site. In many cases, you may find that your Web site has more than one goal.

As you learned in Chapter 3, WorldWide Insurance Brokers, Inc is a large insurance brokerage firm based in Boston. The firm specializes in providing insurance for commercial and industrial clients around the world from Boston and the three branch offices in Toronto, Sydney, and London. The Web site development committee at WorldWide Insurance Brokers, Inc (of which you are a member) has decided that the primary objective for the company's Web site is to provide potential clients an easy way to contact the appropriate branch office. The secondary objectives for the Web site include establishing a corporate image and providing links to related Web pages.

Now that the committee has decided on the Web site's basic goals, it needs to determine the structure and the "look" of the Web site.

8.b Defining the Structure of Your Web Site

Web sites should be structured so users can find important information easily. To keep potential customers from moving on without reading the entire Web page, the information also must be presented in an interesting way. Some Web sites are designed with a single level of separate and unrelated pages to which viewers link directly from the home page. While easy to use, such a flat structure can be boring. Other Web sites have complicated multiple layers of linked pages. Those sites can frustrate potential customers, who are required to link from page to page to find useful information. One way to achieve balance in the structure of a Web site is to limit the number of linked pages and include as much important information as possible in the second or third level of linked pages.

WorldWide's Web site committee has decided that a good way to balance the structure of the company's Web site is to limit it to a home page with links to a separate page for the main office and each branch office. Each office page will have a link to a third-level page that contains links to interesting Web pages featuring the city in which the office is located. Figure 8-1 illustrates the proposed structure of the WorldWide Insurance Brokers, Inc Web site.

FIGURE 8-1

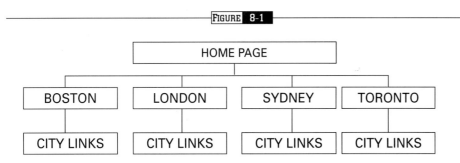

Now that it has determined the structure of the Web site, the committee can design the individual pages.

8.c Designing an Effective Web Page

When viewers browse the Web, they often decide whether to stay at a Web site based on what they immediately see as a Web page loads. Because many viewers read only what they can see as a page is loading and go no further, all important information and links should be positioned as close to the top of the page as possible. To help viewers navigate easily through the pages at a Web site, each page should include links, called **navigational links**, to all the significant pages at the site. For example, you should include a navigational link to the home page on each of the other pages at the Web site.

If a Web page contains large graphic images that are slow to load, some viewers will simply stop the loading process and move on to other Web sites. In addition, some viewers might be using a **text-only browser**, that is, a browser that doesn't read graphic images. For those reasons, you may want to limit the use of graphic images. In general, include them only when they are an important part of the Web page design. For example, you may want to include a company logo that identifies, or "brands," all the pages at your site. If you must use graphic images as links, consider creating an additional text-only version of the page that can be loaded via a link on your home page.

Remember that potential viewers of your Web site reside all over the world. Not only is it difficult to know how they link to your Web pages, you also cannot be certain what Web browser they will be using. To accommodate all the potential viewers of your Web page, design your Web pages so they can be read by a variety of Web browsers. For example, early versions of popular Web browsers like Navigator still are used widely and might not accurately load Web pages designed with new features like frames.

When you are composing the text for your Web page, write as though there were no links in the text. Then go back and designate appropriate text as links. The text links should be meaningful words and phrases, so viewers can scan the links quickly and identify their destinations. Break text into smaller, more manageable pieces to help limit the length of each page. If you have long documents that users may want to print or save, provide separate links to them rather than putting too much text on any one page.

Web pages can contain text, graphics, and links, as well as sound, video, forms to collect data, and links to file servers, called FTP (File Transfer Protocol) sites, for downloading files. At a minimum, a Web page should include the following:

- descriptive information about your company and the purpose of the Web page
- appropriate links to other Web pages or Web sites
- some way to get feedback from viewers
- consistent formatting and use of color and graphic images on all pages to identify them as part of the same Web site

The Web site committee has specified a simple design for the WorldWide Insurance Brokers Inc Web site that incorporates these guidelines:

- Place the company name, addresses, employee names, and e-mail links in the content area of the browser when the Web page loads so the viewer does not have to scroll the page.
- Place links to each branch office page near the top of the home page.
- Place links to the home page and each of the other office pages near the top of each office page.
- Use the same format for all pages.
- Do not use features that can be accessed only by certain browsers (such as frames, blinking, or scrolling text).
- Use the same color scheme and world map graphic logo on all pages.
- Include the names and e-mail addresses of key personnel on each office page.
- Include the corporate e-mail address on each page.

Now that you have the Web site structure and design, you are ready to create a sample home page.

8.d Using HTML to Create Web Pages

You create a Web page using Hypertext Markup Language, or HTML. HTML creates a structured document by defining the parts of a Web page, like the title, headings, body, and graphic images. The HTML codes that label the Web page items are called HTML **tags**. When a browser (like Navigator) reads the Web page, it formats it for the screen based on the HTML tags.

HTML tags are special bracketed text instructions. There are two kinds of HTML tags: **container tags**, which surround and define a Web page item, and **individual tags**, which insert a Web page item. Examples of container tags are **<title>** and **</title>**. The tag **<title>** would appear at the beginning of a title, and the tag **</title>** would appear at the end. The slash character (/) is used in the container tag at the end of a Web page item.

An example of an HTML tag that inserts an item in a Web page is **<p>**, which inserts a paragraph space between items in the body of a Web page.

VIEWING THE HTML SOURCE FOR A WEB PAGE

You can view the HTML tags that structure a Web page by using the Page Source command on the <u>V</u>iew menu in the Navigator window. To load the Online or Offline Companion Web page in the Navigator browser and view the HTML tags and text:

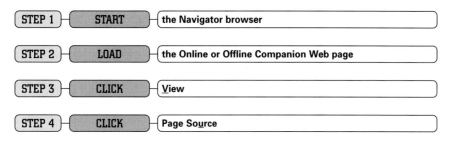

STEP 1	START	the Navigator browser
STEP 2	LOAD	the Online or Offline Companion Web page
STEP 3	CLICK	<u>V</u>iew
STEP 4	CLICK	Page So<u>u</u>rce

The Online or Offline Companion Web page loads in the Source of: window. Your screen should look similar to Figure 8-2.

─── FIGURE 8-2 ───

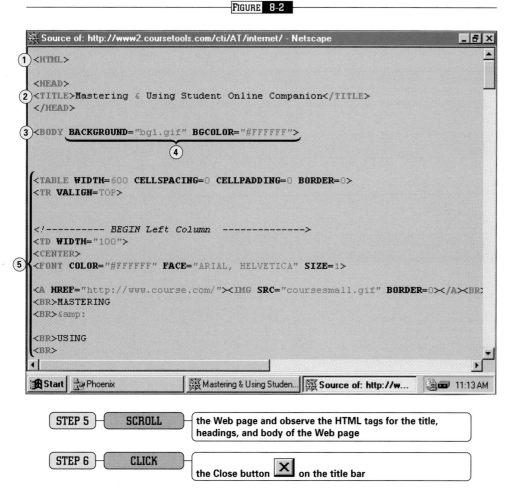

1. Beginning of the HTML document
2. Title that appears in the Navigator title bar
3. Begins the body content
4. Attributes that define the background image and color
5. Other HTML tags that define the structure of the document

| STEP 5 | SCROLL | the Web page and observe the HTML tags for the title, headings, and body of the Web page |
| STEP 6 | CLICK | the Close button [X] on the title bar |

Creating a Home Page

To create a Web page with HTML, you need a text editor that saves files without any font formatting or special characters. For example, you can use text editors like the Windows 95 Notepad accessory or a word processing application like Microsoft Word. You can also use special HTML editors, like Composer, that are specifically designed to create HTML documents. HTML editors contain extra shortcut features to help you insert the appropriate HTML tags in your Web page so you don't have to type them from scratch.

To practice creating WorldWide's Web page, you decide to use Notepad. First, you will enter the HTML tags and text in Notepad and save the document as an HTML file. *For this activity it is important to save your HTML document in the same folder as your student files.* Then you will open the document in Navigator from your hard drive or floppy disk where your student files are stored. Because the Notepad application does not automatically format (or wrap) text so that it appears within left and right margin boundaries, you will open the Notepad application and turn on the Word Wrap feature before you start entering the HTML tags and text:

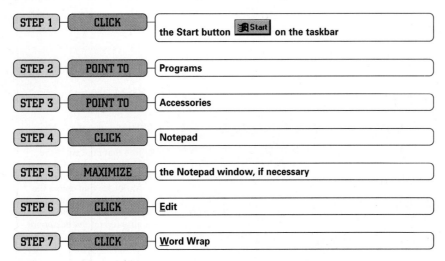

STEP 1	CLICK	the Start button 🔳 Start on the taskbar
STEP 2	POINT TO	Programs
STEP 3	POINT TO	Accessories
STEP 4	CLICK	Notepad
STEP 5	MAXIMIZE	the Notepad window, if necessary
STEP 6	CLICK	Edit
STEP 7	CLICK	Word Wrap

Your screen should look similar to Figure 8-3.

FIGURE 8-3

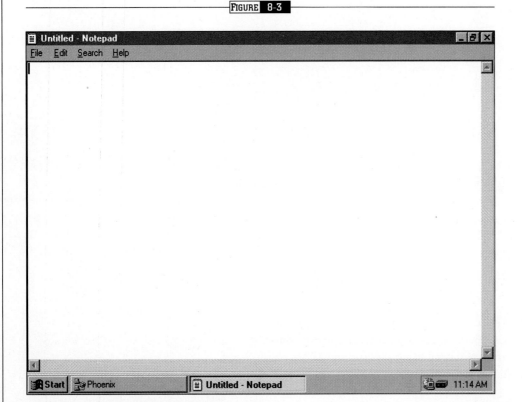

HTML is not case sensitive, which means you can type the tags in either upper-case or lowercase. Also, you use the less-than (<) and greater-than (>) symbols (Shift+comma and Shift+period, respectively) for the brackets. You begin a Web page by typing the container tag **<html>**, which indicates the beginning of an HTML document. After you finish entering all your text and tags, you complete the HTML document by typing **</html>**. To begin the Web page with the <html> tag:

The next step is to create a title for the page that will appear only on the title bar of the browser. The header section of the HTML document is where you define information about the document, like the page title. The header section is defined by <head> container tags. The title text is inside the <title> container tags and is part of the header section of the HTML document. When you use multiple container tags (as in this situation, placing the <title> tags inside the <head> tags), it is important to position the tags in the proper order. Because the title is contained within the header tags and the text is contained within the title tags, you create the header/title in the following order:

1. Type the opening header tag, <head>.
2. Type the opening title tag, <title>.
3. Type the text of the title.
4. Type the closing title tag, </title>.
5. Type the closing header tag, </head>.

To use the <head> and <title> tags to create the title for the WorldWide Insurance Brokers Web page:

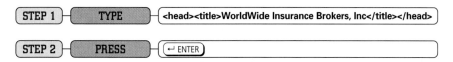

The next step is to begin the page's content (or body) using the **<body>** tag. Certain tags can contain additional formatting instructions called **attributes**. For example, you can define the background color for a Web page by adding the attribute **bgcolor=(name of the color)** to the <body> tag. To begin the body of the Web page and to add a white background color:

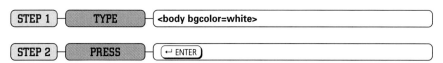

You now need to add the company name as a text heading that appears at the top of the page. You want the text to be centered between the left and right margins and to appear in a large, red font. The **<font>** and **</font>** tags (with color and size attributes) specify text font size and color. The **<center>** and **</center>** tags center items between the left and right margins. You also can use styles to apply a predefined group of formats to text, similar to the styles you use in a word processor. The six HTML styles are defined by the **<h1>** through **<h6>** tags, with <h1> being the top-level style

QUICK TIP

The title you create in Step 1 appears only on the title bar of the browser in which you view the page.

with the largest font. To add a red, centered text heading formatted with the <h1>, or top-level heading style:

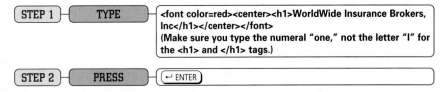

STEP 1 — TYPE — `<font color=red><center><h1>WorldWide Insurance Brokers, Inc</h1></center></font>`
(Make sure you type the numeral "one," not the letter "l" for the <h1> and </h1> tags.)

STEP 2 — PRESS — (↵ ENTER)

Now you need to add the office names and designate them as links to the individual office Web pages. Those links are important and must be positioned below the heading text.

It's easy to organize data (like the office names) by formatting it as table. A **table** is a grid of columns and rows. The intersection of a column and a row is called a **cell**. To organize data using a table, you enter the data in individual cells in the table. In this case, you need a table with one row containing four cells, one for each office name.

The **<table>** and **</table>** HTML tags specify the beginning and the end of a table. You can size the table as a percentage of the screen between the left and right margins. For example, the **width=100%** table attribute extends the table from the left margin to the right margin. You will use this attribute when you define your table.

The **<tr>** and **</tr>** HTML tags define a table row, and the **<td>** and **</td>** HTML tags define the data in each cell. You must define each row and each cell in the table using those tags. The **<a href="(URL or path)">** and **</a>** anchor tags indicate where a linked file is stored. When using those tags, you have the choice of entering just the name of the file or the complete path (disk drive and folder) of the file. If you enter only the name of the linked file (instead of the entire path), you create a "relative" link. A **relative link** establishes a relationship between the page that contains the link and the linked page based on where the pages are stored. If you move the HTML files with relative links to a Web server, the path adjusts to the new location automatically. If you enter the complete path, you create an absolute link. An **absolute link** will always refer to the original disk drive and folder, even when the files are moved to a Web server.

The Notepad folder on your student disk contains four HTML documents to which you will link from the home page: the Web pages for the Boston, Sydney, London, and Toronto offices. You will save the new home page in the Notepad folder with the student files and use relative links.

To begin a table with one row centered between the left and right margins:

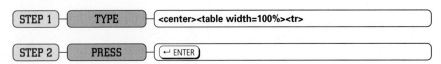

STEP 1 — TYPE — `<center><table width=100%><tr>`

STEP 2 — PRESS — (↵ ENTER)

Now you must define the first cell in the table, the cell that contains the text link to the Boston Web page.

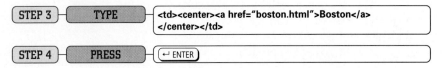

STEP 3 — TYPE — `<td><center><a href="boston.html">Boston</a></center></td>`

STEP 4 — PRESS — (↵ ENTER)

To continue by defining the additional cells for the remaining branch offices:

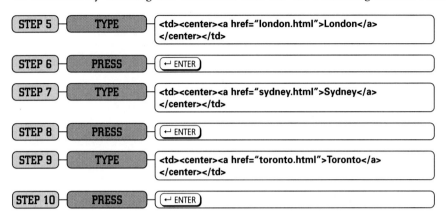

STEP 5	TYPE	`<td><center><a href="london.html">London</a></center></td>`
STEP 6	PRESS	↵ ENTER
STEP 7	TYPE	`<td><center><a href="sydney.html">Sydney</a></center></td>`
STEP 8	PRESS	↵ ENTER
STEP 9	TYPE	`<td><center><a href="toronto.html">Toronto</a></center></td>`
STEP 10	PRESS	↵ ENTER

To close the table:

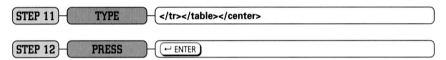

| STEP 11 | TYPE | `</tr></table></center>` |
| STEP 12 | PRESS | ↵ ENTER |

Now you want to add a paragraph space below the table. To insert a paragraph break space:

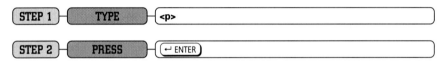

| STEP 1 | TYPE | `<p>` |
| STEP 2 | PRESS | ↵ ENTER |

It is important to include some descriptive text to let the viewer know something about the company and how to contact the company to ask questions and to provide feedback about the Web site. You will add a brief paragraph to do this. To follow the color scheme, you will use a red font.

To add the descriptive paragraph text followed by a paragraph space:

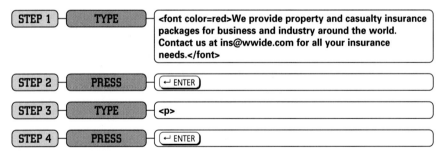

STEP 1	TYPE	`<font color=red>We provide property and casualty insurance packages for business and industry around the world. Contact us at ins@wwide.com for all your insurance needs.</font>`
STEP 2	PRESS	↵ ENTER
STEP 3	TYPE	`<p>`
STEP 4	PRESS	↵ ENTER

Including a company logo on each Web page to identify the pages at your Web site is an effective use of graphic images. You now want to insert your company logo, a graphic image of a world map. There are two types of graphic files used in Web pages today: .gif and .jpg files. The **.gif** (graphic interchange format) files are used for computer-generated graphics. The **.jpg** or (joint picture experts group) files are used for realistic images, like photos. There are many Web sites devoted to providing free, noncopyrighted, graphic-image files that you can download and use. Suppose you found a free graphic image of a world map that you want to use as your logo. This graphic image filename is WORLDCC.GIF and it is located on the student disk. The tag you use to insert an image is **<img src="(path and name of the graphic image file)">.**

A **pixel** is a dot on your monitor or screen identified by an x, y position. The standard 14-inch monitor has a viewing area 640 pixels wide and 480 pixels high. A .gif file can be sized by the number of pixels used to show the graphic image on the screen by using height and width attributes as part of the <img src=> tag. The WORLDCC.GIF file is currently 304 pixels wide and 163 pixels high, which is too large for your home page. You will need to reduce its width to 150 pixels and its height to 50 pixels. You also will use a relative link for the image file.

You can center the image between the left and right margins, as you did with the heading text. To insert the resized and centered WORLDCC.GIF image:

CAUTION

Web pages are protected by copyright laws against unauthorized use of the Web page contents. Be careful not to download and use graphic images (or text) from a copyrighted page without permission.

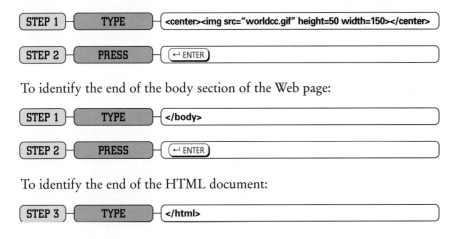

| STEP 1 | TYPE | <img src="worldcc.gif" height=50 width=150> |
| STEP 2 | PRESS | ↵ ENTER |

To identify the end of the body section of the Web page:

| STEP 1 | TYPE | </body> |
| STEP 2 | PRESS | ↵ ENTER |

To identify the end of the HTML document:

| STEP 3 | TYPE | </html> |

After you have finished entering the HTML tags, text, graphics, and links, you must save the Web page as a text file with an HTML file extension. The file extension identifies the file as a Web page. You will save your HTML document along with your student files, in the Notepad folder. That folder contains the office Web pages and the WORLDCC.GIF graphic image. To save the HTML document:

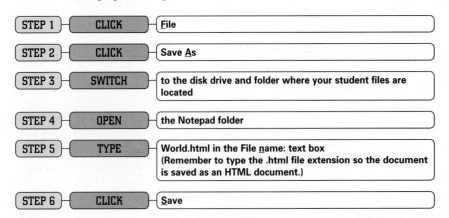

STEP 1	CLICK	File
STEP 2	CLICK	Save As
STEP 3	SWITCH	to the disk drive and folder where your student files are located
STEP 4	OPEN	the Notepad folder
STEP 5	TYPE	World.html in the File name: text box (Remember to type the .html file extension so the document is saved as an HTML document.)
STEP 6	CLICK	Save

Your screen should look similar to Figure 8-4. If your text does not wrap between the margins like Figure 8-4, click the Edit command and verify that the Word Wrap command has a check mark beside it to indicate it is turned on. Even if Word Wrap is turned on, the text on your screen may be aligned differently than in the figure.

FIGURE 8-4

```
world - Notepad
File   Edit   Search   Help
<html>
<head><title>WorldWide Insurance Brokers, Inc</title></head>
<body bgcolor=white>
<font color=red><center><h1>WorldWide Insurance Brokers,
Inc</h1></center></font>
<center><table width=100%><tr>
<td><center><a href="boston.html">Boston</a></center></td>
<td><center><a href="london.html">London</a></center></td>
<td><center><a href="sydney.html">Sydney</a></center></td>
<td><center><a href="toronto.html">Toronto</a></center></td>
</tr></table></center>
<p>
<font color=red>We provide property and casualty insurance packages for
business and industry around the world. Contact us at ins@wwide.com for all
your insurance needs.</font>
<p>
<center><img src="worldcc.gif" height=50 width=150></center>
</body>
</html>
```

Start   Phoenix   WorldWide Insurance Bro...   world - Notepad   9:06 AM

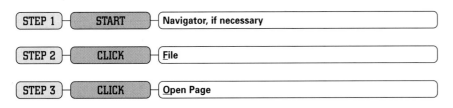

STEP 7 — CLICK — the Close button [X] on the the Notepad title bar

Now that you have created and saved the Web page, you are ready to view it in the Navigator browser.

Viewing a Web Page Stored at Your Computer

The WORLD.HTML Web page file is a **local file,** which means it is stored at your computer rather than on a Web server maintained by your ISP. You already may have experience using another example of a local file, the Offline Companion.

To view the file, you will start Navigator and then open the Web page from the appropriate drive and folder on your computer where the student files are stored. To view the WORLD.HTML Web page:

STEP 1 — START — Navigator, if necessary

STEP 2 — CLICK — File

STEP 3 — CLICK — Open Page

CAUTION

Because you are using relative links in your Web page, WORLD.HTML must be saved in the same student file folder as the branch office pages and the WORLDCC.GIF image file. If you save the WORLD.HTML file in a different location, the links on your branch office pages will not work.

The Open Page dialog box opens. You will use this dialog box to locate the WORLD.HTML file stored on the student disk.

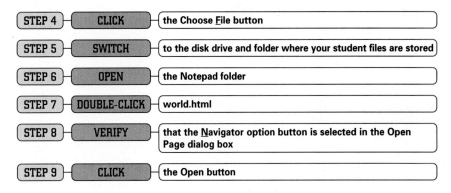

STEP 4	CLICK	the Choose File button
STEP 5	SWITCH	to the disk drive and folder where your student files are stored
STEP 6	OPEN	the Notepad folder
STEP 7	DOUBLE-CLICK	world.html
STEP 8	VERIFY	that the Navigator option button is selected in the Open Page dialog box
STEP 9	CLICK	the Open button

Your Web page appears in the content area of the Navigator browser. Your screen should look similar to Figure 8-5.

FIGURE 8-5

If your Web page does not look similar to Figure 8-5, open the WORLD.HTML document in the Notepad application and compare your HTML tags and text with Figure 8-4. If you do not use the correct format for HTML tags, as shown in Figure 8-4, your Web page will not look like Figure 8-5. Make any necessary corrections, save the corrected WORLD.HTML document, and open it again in Navigator for review. If necessary, continue to make corrections and view the page in Navigator until your screen looks similar to Figure 8-5.

You can view, but not edit, the HTML source code with the Page Source command on the <u>V</u>iew menu. To view the HTML source code for the WorldWide Insurance Brokers, Inc home page:

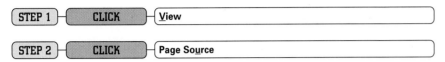

STEP 1 — **CLICK** — <u>V</u>iew

STEP 2 — **CLICK** — Page So<u>u</u>rce

Notice that the HTML tags in the document appear in a different color than the text. Your screen should look similar to Figure 8-6.

FIGURE 8-6

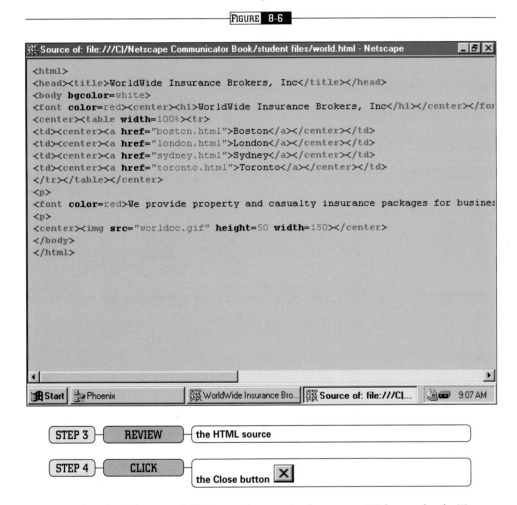

```
Source of: file:///C|/Netscape Communicator Book/student files/world.html - Netscape

<html>
<head><title>WorldWide Insurance Brokers, Inc</title></head>
<body bgcolor=white>
<font color=red><center><h1>WorldWide Insurance Brokers, Inc</h1></center></fon
<center><table width=100%><tr>
<td><center><a href="boston.html">Boston</a></center></td>
<td><center><a href="london.html">London</a></center></td>
<td><center><a href="sydney.html">Sydney</a></center></td>
<td><center><a href="toronto.html">Toronto</a></center></td>
</tr></table></center>
<p>
<font color=red>We provide property and casualty insurance packages for busines
<p>
<center><img src="worldcc.gif" height=50 width=150></center>
</body>
</html>
```

Start | Phoenix | WorldWide Insurance Bro... | Source of: file:///C|... | 9:07 AM

STEP 3 — **REVIEW** — the HTML source

STEP 4 — **CLICK** — the Close button ☒

You also should test each link to make certain the correct Web page loads. To test your link to the Boston office Web page:

STEP 1 — **CLICK** — the <u>Boston</u> link

The Boston Web page appears.

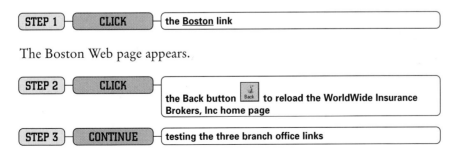

STEP 2 — **CLICK** — the Back button to reload the WorldWide Insurance Brokers, Inc home page

STEP 3 — **CONTINUE** — testing the three branch office links

If any of your office links do not load the appropriate page, open the WORLD.HTML document in the Notepad application, make any necessary changes, save the document with the changes, and open it again in the Navigator browser. If necessary, continue to make corrections until the office links are working correctly.

You've just created a Web page the hard way, by typing all the text and HTML tags. In the process, you've gained some understanding of how HTML defines the parts of a Web page. Now you will learn how to create a web page the easy way, using Netscape Composer, an HTML editor that automatically inserts the correct HTML tags for you.

8.e   Using Composer to Create Web Pages

Composer is an HTML editor that contains shortcuts to inserting the HTML tags needed to create a Web page. You will use Composer to re-create the home page for WorldWide Insurance Brokers, Inc. Composer allows you to create the page without manually entering the HTML tags needed to define and structure the page.

To start Composer:

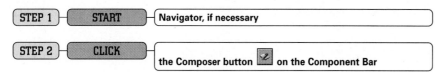

STEP 1 — START → Navigator, if necessary

STEP 2 — CLICK → the Composer button on the Component Bar

QUICK TIP
Many Web sites offer helpful information on using HTML to create Web pages. For more information on using HTML to create Web pages, try searching the Web for "HTML tutorials."

MENU TIP
You can start the Composer application from inside Navigator by clicking the Page Composer command on the Communicator menu.

CAUTION
If the Component Bar is not visible, click the Show Component Bar command on the Communicator menu.

The Netscape Composer window opens with a blank HTML document. Your screen should look similar to Figure 8-7.

FIGURE 8-7

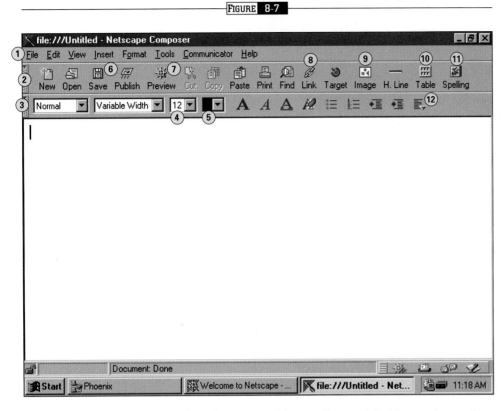

1. Menu bar
2. Composition toolbar
3. Formatting toolbar
4. Font Size box
5. Font Color box
6. Save button
7. Preview button
8. Link button
9. Image button
10. Table button
11. Spelling button
12. Alignment button

Composer contains a menu bar, the Composition toolbar, and the Formatting toolbar. You will use the buttons on the toolbars and commands from the menu bar to insert the appropriate HTML tags as you create the Web page. (The buttons you will use later in this chapter are marked in the figure.)

Just like the Web page you created in the previous section, this page will have a title, a formatted text heading, a table containing the office names as links, a formatted descriptive paragraph, and a graphic image. To add a title to the Web page:

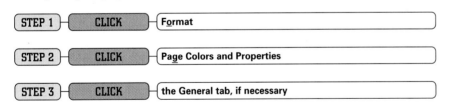

STEP 1	CLICK	Format
STEP 2	CLICK	Page Colors and Properties
STEP 3	CLICK	the General tab, if necessary

The General tab in the Page Properties dialog box opens. Your screen should look similar to Figure 8-8.

FIGURE 8-8

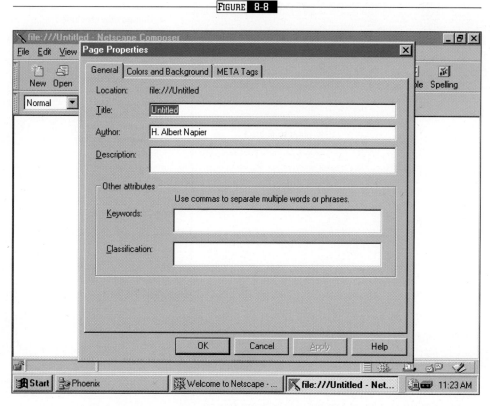

You can add a title, author name, description, and other page attributes (e.g., background color) in this dialog box. Because the background color default is white, you only need to add a title. To identify the author of the page, you also can add your name. For information on the other options in this dialog box, click the dialog box Help button. To create a title and add your name:

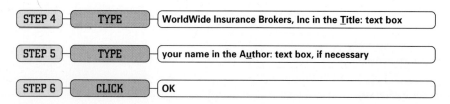

STEP 4	TYPE	WorldWide Insurance Brokers, Inc in the Title: text box
STEP 5	TYPE	your name in the Author: text box, if necessary
STEP 6	CLICK	OK

Observe the new title on the Composer title bar. Next, you want to create a formatted text heading to appear at the top of the page. You format text in Composer the same way you format text in a word processor, by selecting the text and clicking a toolbar button or a menu command.

To center and format the company name as a text heading:

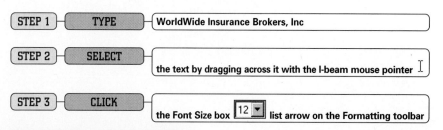

STEP 1	TYPE	WorldWide Insurance Brokers, Inc
STEP 2	SELECT	the text by dragging across it with the I-beam mouse pointer
STEP 3	CLICK	the Font Size box 12 list arrow on the Formatting toolbar

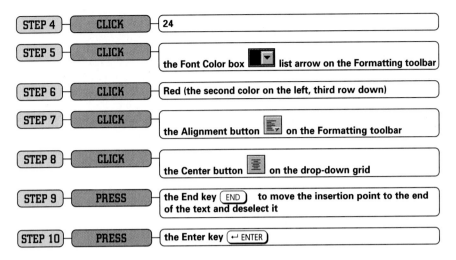

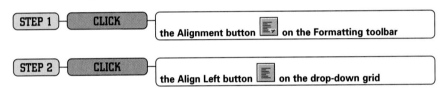

Notice that the insertion point is still centered below the heading text. To position the insertion point at the left margin:

Your screen should look similar to Figure 8-9.

FIGURE 8-9

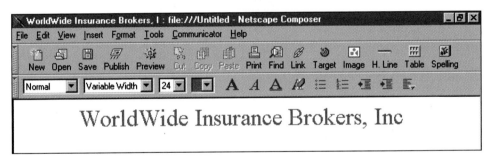

You will use a table to organize the links to the separate offices, just as you did when you created the Web page in Notepad. To create the table:

The New Table Properties dialog box opens. Your screen should look similar to Figure 8-10.

FIGURE 8-10

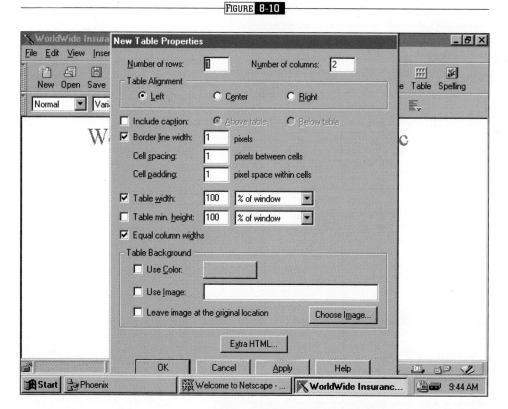

You use the New Table Properties dialog box to define the number of rows and the number of columns in your table and to set formatting attributes. In this case, you want a table with one row and four columns. To define the rows and columns:

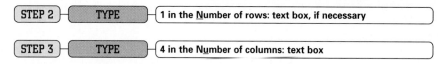

STEP 2	TYPE	1 in the Number of rows: text box, if necessary

STEP 3	TYPE	4 in the Number of columns: text box

To center the table between the left and right margins, set the table width, remove the table border, and specify equal column widths:

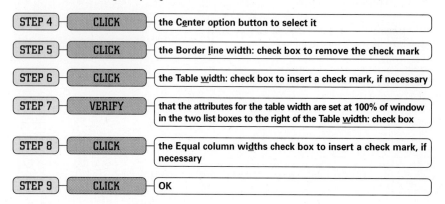

STEP 4	CLICK	the Center option button to select it

STEP 5	CLICK	the Border line width: check box to remove the check mark

STEP 6	CLICK	the Table width: check box to insert a check mark, if necessary

STEP 7	VERIFY	that the attributes for the table width are set at 100% of window in the two list boxes to the right of the Table width: check box

STEP 8	CLICK	the Equal column widths check box to insert a check mark, if necessary

STEP 9	CLICK	OK

A table consisting of one row and four columns appears. The dotted gridlines around the border of the table are for your reference and will not appear on the Web page when it is viewed in a browser. Your screen should look similar to Figure 8-11.

FIGURE 8-11

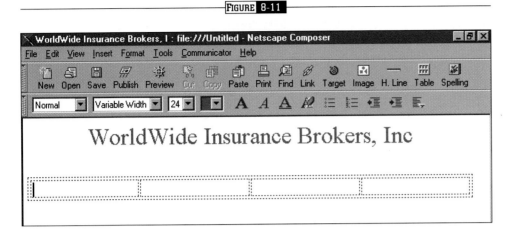

Before entering text in the table, you will take a moment to save the Web page. As you work on a Web page, it is a good idea to save it frequently. You will save this HTML document in the Composer folder where your student files are stored. The Composer folder contains the separate office Web pages and the WORLD.GIF file for the Composer activity. To save the Web page:

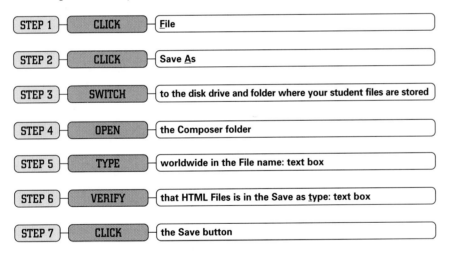

STEP 1 — CLICK — File

STEP 2 — CLICK — Save As

STEP 3 — SWITCH — to the disk drive and folder where your student files are stored

STEP 4 — OPEN — the Composer folder

STEP 5 — TYPE — worldwide in the File name: text box

STEP 6 — VERIFY — that HTML Files is in the Save as type: text box

STEP 7 — CLICK — the Save button

To enter the data in the table, you will simply type the name of each office in a cell of the table. After entering the office names, you will center the text in each cell for a more attractive presentation. Finally, you will format the text by changing its color and size. To add the office names to the table:

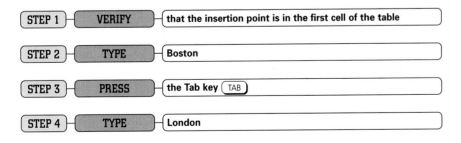

STEP 1 — VERIFY — that the insertion point is in the first cell of the table

STEP 2 — TYPE — Boston

STEP 3 — PRESS — the Tab key (TAB)

STEP 4 — TYPE — London

STEP 5	PRESS	TAB

STEP 6	TYPE	Sydney

STEP 7	PRESS	TAB

STEP 8	TYPE	Toronto

To center the contents of the cells and to change the font color:

STEP 1	SELECT	the table cells by dragging across the cells with the I-beam mouse pointer

STEP 2	CLICK	the Alignment button on the Formatting toolbar

STEP 3	CLICK	the Center button on the drop-down grid

STEP 4	CLICK	the Font Color box list arrow on the Formatting toolbar

STEP 5	CLICK	Blue (second from the right, fourth row down)

STEP 6	CLICK	the Font Size box 12 list arrow on the Formatting toolbar

STEP 7	CLICK	18

STEP 8	CLICK	in the white background area to deselect the contents of the table cells

Your screen should look similar to Figure 8-12.

FIGURE 8-12

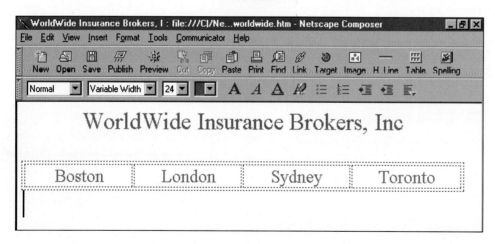

Before you continue, you should save the Web page again.

STEP 9	CLICK	the Save button on the Composition toolbar

Now you need to designate the table text as links to the separate office Web pages. To create the link to the Boston office Web page:

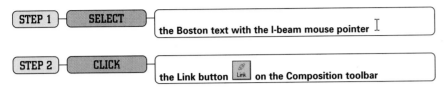

STEP 1 — **SELECT** — the Boston text with the I-beam mouse pointer I

STEP 2 — **CLICK** — the Link button [Link] on the Composition toolbar

The Link tab in the Character Properties dialog box opens. Your screen should look similar to Figure 8-13.

FIGURE 8-13

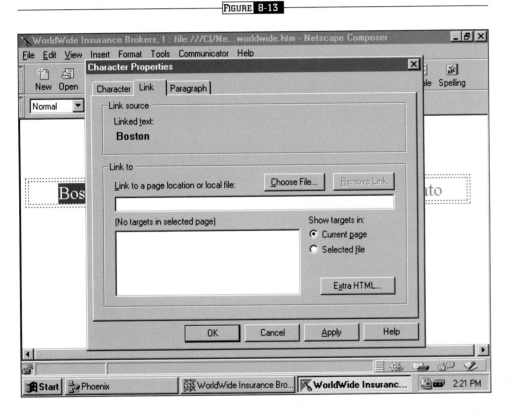

You will create the link path to the BOSTON.HTML file in this dialog box. The home page and the linked pages are stored in the same folder and will be moved together to the ISP, so you should create a relative link, that is, a link that includes only the file name. To create a relative link to the Boston Web page:

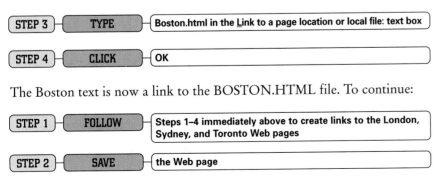

STEP 3 — **TYPE** — Boston.html in the Link to a page location or local file: text box

STEP 4 — **CLICK** — OK

The Boston text is now a link to the BOSTON.HTML file. To continue:

STEP 1 — **FOLLOW** — Steps 1–4 immediately above to create links to the London, Sydney, and Toronto Web pages

STEP 2 — **SAVE** — the Web page

Now you are ready to preview the Web page to see how it will look in the Navigator browser. To preview the Web page:

The WORLDWIDE.HTML Web page opens in the Navigator window. You decide to review the page contents so far and test the links to the separate office pages.

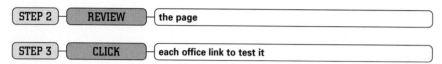

After you have finished testing the links, you will close the Navigator window and return to the Composer window to continue creating the page.

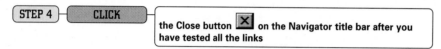

If there is an error on the page or with the links, make corrections before you continue. For example, if a link is not working, select the office name in the table and recreate the link. To reposition the insertion point:

Next, you'll create the paragraph describing WorldWide Insurance Brokers. After you have entered and formatted the paragraph text, you will save and preview the Web page. To add the paragraph text:

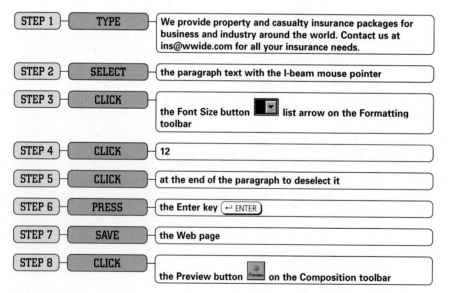

Now that you've finished previewing the Web page, you can close the Navigator window and return to Composer.

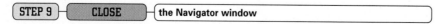

As you create a Web page in Composer, you see the text without the HTML tags you used to format it. In some cases, though, you may need to insert HTML tags into the Web page. For example, suppose you want to insert a paragraph space after the paragraph text and before you insert the logo graphic image. There is no button on the toolbars to insert the <p> tag. To practice inserting HTML tags in your Web page, you will use the HTML command on the Insert menu to insert the <p> tag. To insert a paragraph space:

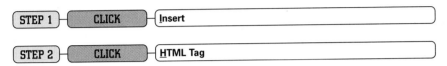

The HTML Tag dialog box opens. Your screen should look similar to Figure 8-14.

FIGURE 8-14

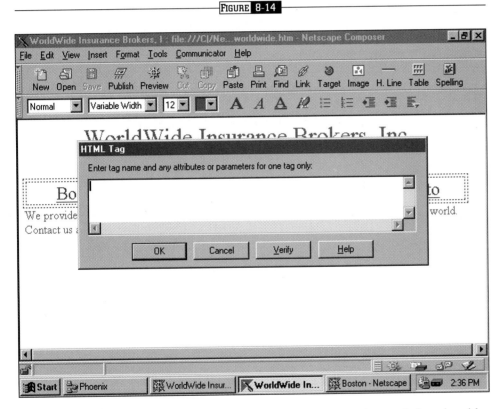

You create HTML tags in this dialog box. To insert a paragraph space below the table:

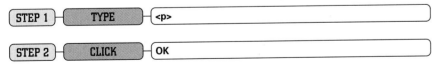

An icon indicating the HTML tag is inserted in the Web page.

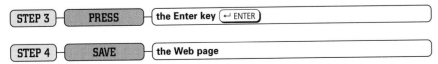

When you place your mouse pointer over the HTML tag icon, a yellow flag appears containing the HTML tag.

STEP 5 — MOVE — the mouse pointer to the HTML tag icon

Your screen should look similar to Figure 8-15.

FIGURE 8-15

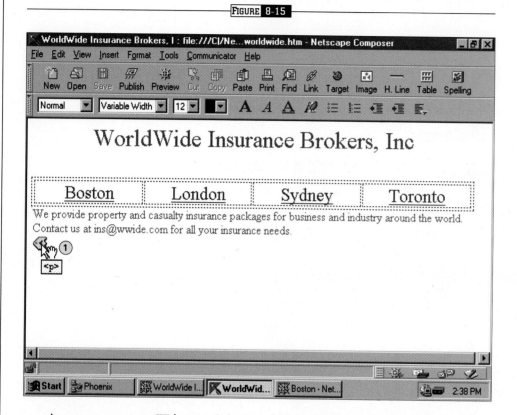

1. HTML tag

As you create your Web page, it is a good idea to preview the page frequently to see how your additions and changes will look in the Navigator browser. To practice previewing your Web page:

STEP 1 — PREVIEW — the Web page

STEP 2 — CLOSE — the Navigator window to return to the Composer window

The last step is to insert and center the graphic image logo below the paragraph text.

STEP 1 — CLICK — the Image button [Image] on the Composition toolbar

The Image tab in the Image Properties dialog box opens. Your screen should look similar to Figure 8-16.

FIGURE 8-16

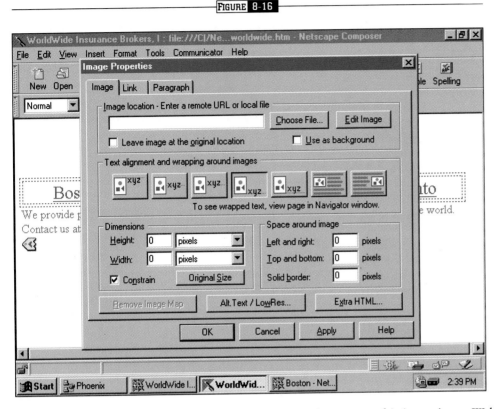

Using the Image Properties dialog box, you can insert a graphic image into a Web page, edit a graphic image, and attach a link to a graphic image. In this case, you will insert and size the WORLDCC.GIF graphic image. To insert and size the WORLDCC.GIF graphic image:

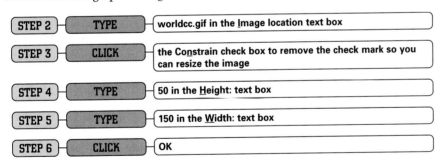

STEP 2	TYPE	worldcc.gif in the Image location text box
STEP 3	CLICK	the Constrain check box to remove the check mark so you can resize the image
STEP 4	TYPE	50 in the Height: text box
STEP 5	TYPE	150 in the Width: text box
STEP 6	CLICK	OK

The WORLDCC.GIF image is inserted at the left margin next to the new paragraph tag. To center the image:

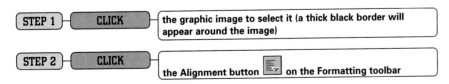

| STEP 1 | CLICK | the graphic image to select it (a thick black border will appear around the image) |
| STEP 2 | CLICK | the Alignment button on the Formatting toolbar |

QUICK TIP

To learn more about other options in the Image Properties dialog box, click the Help button.

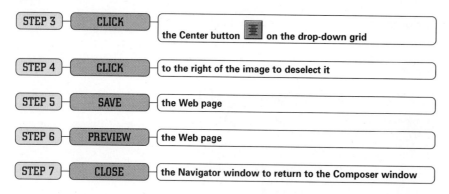

The WorldWide Insurance Brokers, Inc home page now looks like the home page you created in Notepad. You will add one extra item to this version of the page. In addition to listing the company's e-mail address in the paragraph text, you will create a link to the e-mail address text that automatically opens the e-mail composition window of the viewer's browser. That encourages viewers to contact you about your products and services.

To create an e-mail link:

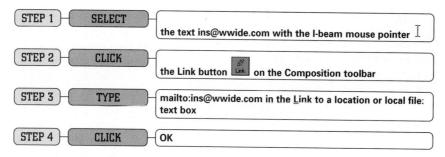

The selected text becomes a link. Next, you will save the Web page and then preview it to test the link.

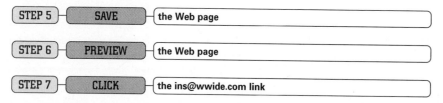

The Composition window opens, and the ins@wwide.com e-mail address automatically appears in the To: text box.

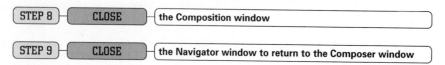

After you create a Web page, you should test it before transferring it to a Web server.

8.f Testing Your Web Pages

Remember, not all viewers will be using the Navigator browser. Therefore, it is important to test the "look" of your Web pages by previewing them in different browsers, if possible. If you have access to another browser, use it to open the WorldWide Insurance Brokers, Inc home page and observe any differences between how the home page looks in Navigator and in the other browser.

The next step in testing your Web page is to check the spelling. To check the spelling of the WorldWide Insurance Brokers, Inc home page:

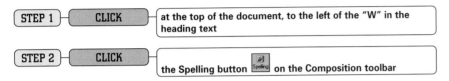

| STEP 1 | CLICK | at the top of the document, to the left of the "W" in the heading text |
| STEP 2 | CLICK | the Spelling button [Spelling] on the Composition toolbar |

The Check Spelling dialog box opens. Your screen should look similar to Figure 8-17.

FIGURE 8-17

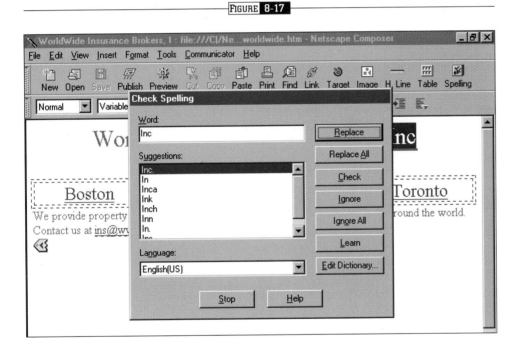

The Composer spelling feature works like the spelling feature in a word processing program. It highlights words that are not included in its built-in dictionary and suggests a substitute word when possible. You can choose to ignore the word if it is correctly spelled, correct the word manually, or accept the substitute word. The first word highlighted is "Inc" without a period. This is the preferred spelling and punctuation for the company's name. To ignore the word "Inc":

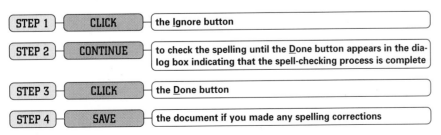

STEP 1	CLICK	the Ignore button
STEP 2	CONTINUE	to check the spelling until the Done button appears in the dialog box indicating that the spell-checking process is complete
STEP 3	CLICK	the Done button
STEP 4	SAVE	the document if you made any spelling corrections

The next step in testing your work is to try all the links at the Web site. You already have tested the links on the home page. You should now preview the home page, click the Boston office link to load the Boston Web page, and test the links on the Boston Web page. To test the Boston link on the home page:

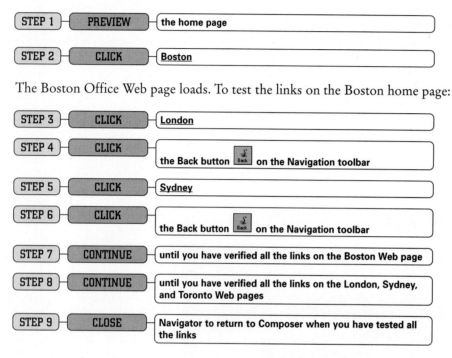

| STEP 1 | PREVIEW | the home page |
| STEP 2 | CLICK | Boston |

The Boston Office Web page loads. To test the links on the Boston home page:

STEP 3	CLICK	London
STEP 4	CLICK	the Back button on the Navigation toolbar
STEP 5	CLICK	Sydney
STEP 6	CLICK	the Back button on the Navigation toolbar
STEP 7	CONTINUE	until you have verified all the links on the Boston Web page
STEP 8	CONTINUE	until you have verified all the links on the London, Sydney, and Toronto Web pages
STEP 9	CLOSE	Navigator to return to Composer when you have tested all the links

The final stage of testing your Web page is to have several people (both inside and outside your organization) review it. Weigh their suggestions carefully and revise your Web pages as necessary. Then when your Web pages are finally finished, you can make them available on the Web by placing them on a Web server. You'll learn how to do that in the next section.

8.g Publishing Your Web Pages

The process of transferring your Web pages to a Web server is called **publishing.** You can publish the home page you just created using Composer's FTP program. (As you learned in Chapter 1, an FTP program is used to transfer files on the Internet.) The FTP program allows you to send, or **upload**, all your Web pages (the HTML files and related graphics files) to an ISP, where they will be placed in a folder on a Web server. Because it is important to store your Web pages and graphic files together, make sure all your files are stored in the same folder. Once they are stored on the Web server, your Web pages are available to Web users around the world.

The exact steps involved in uploading Web pages will vary from one ISP to another. Before attempting to upload any files, call or e-mail your ISP and ask the technical support personnel for instructions. In the following steps you will prepare to upload the files; however, because you do not have access to a Web server, you will *not* complete the uploading process.

To begin uploading the WORLDWIDE.HTML file and other related files from the student disk:

The Publish: dialog box opens. Your screen should look similar to Figure 8-18.

FIGURE 8-18

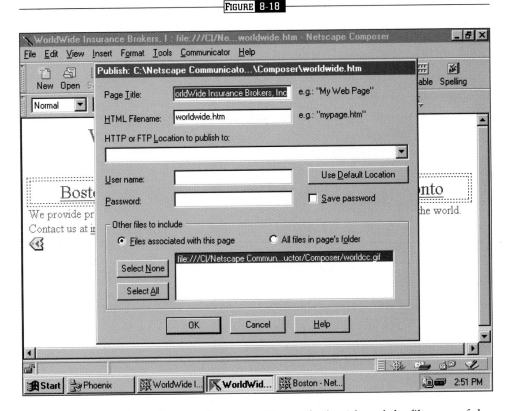

To upload all the Web pages, first you will specify the title and the filename of the home page and the Web server where the files will be located.

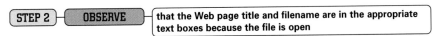

User names and passwords protect access to most file servers. Your ISP will have provided you with the appropriate Web site location, user name, and password to enter in the dialog box. To enter the Web site location, user name, and password:

| STEP 3 | TYPE | ftp.xeon.com in the HTTP or FTP Location to publish to: text box |

| STEP 4 | TYPE | your name in the User name: text box |

| STEP 5 | TYPE | XXXXX in the Password: text box |

Because there are several HTML files and image files for your Web site, you want to upload the entire contents of the Composer folder on the student disk.

| STEP 6 | CLICK | the All files in page's folder option button |

Your screen should look similar to Figure 8-19.

FIGURE 8-19

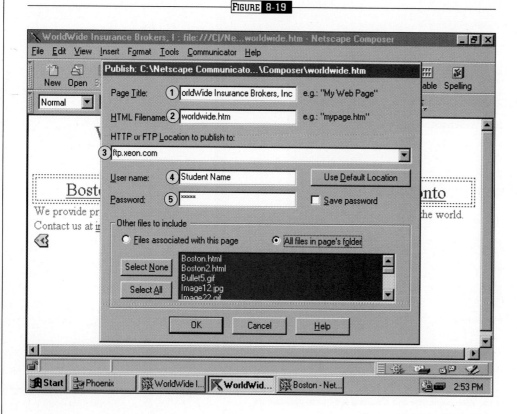

1. Web page title
2. Web page filename
3. FTP location
4. User name
5. Password

Remember, you do not have access to a Web server so you *cannot actually upload the files*. You will close the dialog box and then close Composer and Navigator:

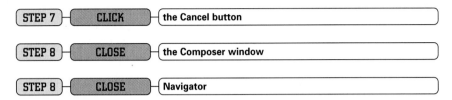

STEP 7	CLICK	the Cancel button
STEP 8	CLOSE	the Composer window
STEP 8	CLOSE	Navigator

After you have uploaded your Web pages to a Web server, you should think about ways to get your new Web site noticed. In the next section you will learn some ways to do just that.

8.h Getting Your Web Site Noticed

There are many ways to let people who browse the Web know about your site. For starters, you can register your Web site with a directory like Galaxy. To do that, go to the directory you're interested in and look for a link for new Web sites. It's also important to have links to your Web site included on other sites. When you find other Web pages that might logically link to your Web site, you can send an e-mail message to the person who maintains the other Web site (called a Webmaster) and ask that person to add a link to your site. Also, you can add your home page URL to your company print media advertising, company letterhead, business cards, and fax cover sheets.

QUICK TIP

There are a number of companies devoted to promoting commercial Web sites. To find those companies on the Web, try searching for "web site promotion."

Summary

> The primary reason most companies want to establish a Web page is to advertise their products and services.

> At the very least, a company's Web page should include the company name, a brief descriptive paragraph about the company, any appropriate links, and a way to get feedback.

> You create a Web page using the Hypertext Markup Language (HTML).

> HTML tags are special bracketed codes that define the structure of a Web page.

> You can create a Web page in a text editor, like Notepad; a word processor; or a special HTML editor, like Composer.

> Special HTML editors, like Composer, insert most of the HTML tags for you automatically.

> You must upload your Web pages and related graphics to a file server maintained by an ISP to make your Web pages available on the Web. This is known as publishing your Web pages.

> You can tell others about your Web page by listing it with a directory, asking Webmasters to add a link to your page on their home pages, and adding your home page URL to your company's printed materials.

Commands Review

ACTION	MENU BAR	SHORTCUT MENU	MOUSE	KEYBOARD
Add a title to a Web page in Composer	Format, Page Colors and Properties			ALT+O, G
Insert an HTML tag in Composer	Insert, HTML tag			ALT+I, H
Load a Web page stored at your computer	File, Open Page			ALT+F, O
Load Composer	Communicator, Page Composer			ALT+C, P
Open Notepad	Start, Programs, Accessories, Notepad			
Preview a Web page in Composer			Preview	
Publish a Web page from Composer	File, Publish		Publish	ALT+F, U
View a Web page with HTML tags	View, Page Source			ALT+V, U

Concepts Review

Circle the correct answer.

1. When creating a Web page, you should assume that viewers will:
[a] read all text that appears on a lengthy Web page.
[b] wait a long time to load a large graphic image.
[c] evaluate your Web site based on what is immediately visible as the Web page loads.
[d] avoid navigational links.

2. Web pages are created using:
[a] HTTP.
[b] HTML.
[c] FTP.
[d] TCP/IP.

3. A container tag:
[a] surrounds and defines a Web page item.
[b] inserts a Web page item.
[c] marks the end of a Web page.
[d] inserts paragraph space between items in the body of a Web page.

4. Formatting instructions added to a tag are called:
[a] attributes.
[b] links.
[c] body.
[d] titles.

5. If you move an HTML file and the path adjusts to the new location automatically, the link is:
[a] absolute.
[b] text.
[c] table.
[d] relative.

6. A file type commonly used for computer-generated graphics is:
[a] .pixel.
[b] .gif.
[c] .jpg.
[d] .img.

7. A local file is stored at:
[a] your computer.
[b] a Web server maintained by your ISP.
[c] an HTML source file.
[d] a Web site.

8. The process of transferring your Web pages to a Web server is called:
[a] uploading.
[b] composing.
[c] loading.
[d] publishing.

9. Which is not an appropriate method of advising others about your Web page?
[a] registering your Web site with a directory like Galaxy.
[b] adding your URL to any printed media.
[c] sending e-mail to everyone in an online directory telling them about your Web page.
[d] sending e-mail to a Webmaster asking that a link be added for your URL to his/her Web page.

Circle [T] if the statement is true or [F] if the statement is false.

1. [T] [F] A text-only browser displays graphic images.

2. [T] [F] The slash character (/) is always used in the container tag at the beginning of a Web page item.

3. [T] [F] HTML is case sensitive so you must be careful when you type in capital letters.

4. [T] [F] Once you create a Web page, you cannot edit it.

5. [T] [F] The header section of the HTML document is where you define information about the document like the title page.

6. [T] [F] The title tag inserts text in the title bar of the Web browser.

SCANS

7. (T) (F) HTML text editors contain shortcuts for inserting HTML tags.

8. (T) (F) Because public relations is not usually a primary purpose of a Web page, a company does not need to be concerned about the image it portrays on a Web page.

9. (T) (F) To save time and prevent errors, you can copy and paste lines of text and tags in Notepad and then edit them as needed.

10. (T) (F) It does not matter in what order you position HTML tags when creating a Web page.

Fill in the blank to complete the sentence.

1. _____ creates a structured document by defining the parts of a Web page, such as the title, headings, body, or graphic images.

2. The <p> tag inserts a(n) _____.

3. To create a Web page with HTML, you can use a special HTML editor like Composer or a(n) _____ editor.

4. You begin a Web page by typing the container tag _____.

5. The <tr> and </tr> HTML tags define a(n) _____.

6. A(n) _____ link will always refer to the original disk drive and folder of the linked Web page even when the files are moved to another location.

7. _____ files are used for realistic images like photos.

8. A(n) _____ is a dot on your monitor or screen identified by an x,y position.

9. Composer's FTP program allows you to _____ all of your Web pages to an ISP.

10. The person who maintains a Web site is called a(n) _____.

Case Problems

PROBLEM 1: COMMUNICATE YOUR IDEAS

Complete this problem using your ISP connection and the Internet.

In preparation for creating your own Web pages, you decide to go online and review some existing Web pages. Start Navigator and browse the Web looking for three examples of Web pages you think are effective and three that you think are not very good. Print these six Web pages, close Navigator, and then analyze these pages for content, organization, design, and effectiveness. For each Web page, write a paragraph that answers the following questions: What are the goals of the page or site? Did the Web page achieve these goals? What do you like or dislike about the page? What elements work or don't work? Why do you think the page is effective or ineffective?

PROBLEM 2: HELP

Complete this problem using Composer and the Online Help system.

You manage Images, an art shop that sells lithographs of original paintings and drawings. The owner wants to start advertising the available lithographs on the Web to enable potential customers around the world to see most current lithographs available at any time. He thinks the best way to do this is to place graphic images of each lithograph on the Web page. You have heard that good Web page construction limits the size of graphic images to reduce the time it takes a page to load. However, small "thumbnail" images will not show the detail and richness of the lithographs. You decide to consult the online Help system to find a solution to this problem.

Start Composer. Use the <u>H</u>elp Contents command on the <u>H</u>elp menu to open online Help. Read the Help topics "Doing Graphics Justice" and "Working with Images." Then answer these questions. What is the recommended total file size Netscape recommends for images on a single Web page? What is one way you can keep the image file sizes small on your primary Web page, yet still provide access to larger, more detailed images?

PROBLEM 3

Complete this problem using Composer and the Online Companion.

As the manager of a new and used music store, you plan to advertise your large collection of hard-to-find "golden oldies" records and cassettes on the Web. Create your Web page in Notepad using fictitious information. Make sure you include a title, a centered major heading, two paragraphs of body text that are formatted with various color and size attributes, and a link to a related Web site. (Hint: use a search engine to locate an appropriate music site.) Save the HTML document as Records.html in a new folder named Music. Create a second page that includes a list of titles and artists organized in a table; format the text appropriately. Save the second page as Artists.html, in the Music folder. Create a link from the first page to the second page and a link from the second page back to the first. Open the local file in Navigator, review the pages, and test all your links. Make edits and corrections to your HTML documents in Notepad as necessary until you're satisfied with how the pages look. Print the finished Web pages from Navigator, then print the source pages from Notepad.

PROBLEM 4

You own a small greenhouse that specializes in exotic plants. You want to advertise your store and greenhouse on the Web to inform potential customers about your plants. Create your Web page in Composer using fictitious information. Make sure you include a title, a centered major heading, three paragraphs of body text that are formatted with various color and size attributes, and a link to a related Web site. (Hint: use a search engine to locate an appropriate plant site.) Also, insert the company's e-mail address and then create a link from the company's e-mail address text that automatically opens the e-mail composition window of the viewer's browser. Save the HTML document as Plants.html, in a new folder named Greenhouse. Create a second page that includes a list of exotic plants and prices organized in a table; format the text appropriately. Save the second page as Prices.html, in the Greenhouse folder. Create a link from the first page to the second page and a link from the second page back to the first. Preview the document in Navigator and test all your links. Make edits and corrections as necessary until you're satisfied with the pages. Print the finished Web pages from Navigator. Then print the source pages from Composer.

Getting Online Help

Appendix Overview

Netscape provides extensive online information to help you use and maintain the Communicator Internet suite software. In this appendix you will learn how to get help for each individual Communicator application and how to load updates to the Communicator software.

SNAPSHOT

In this appendix you will learn to:

> **Get online Help for Navigator, Messenger, Collabra, and Composer**

> **Load Communicator software updates with SmartUpdate**

IN THIS APPENDIX

You must be connected to your ISP to be able to complete the hands-on activities in this appendix.

A.a Getting Online Help for Navigator, Messenger, Collabra, and Composer

One of the best ways to learn more about the different features in each of Communicator's applications is to review the online Help provided for each application. You can access online Help by clicking the Help menu on the menu bar in the Welcome to Netscape (Navigator), the Inbox (Messenger), the Message Center (Collabra), or the Composer window. To start Navigator and view the Help menu:

| STEP 1 | START | Navigator from the Start menu or the desktop icon |

| STEP 2 | CLICK | Help |

The Help menu appears. Your screen should look similar to Figure A-1.

FIGURE A-1

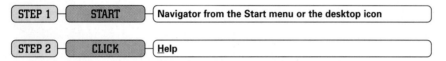

The Help menu offers numerous options for help on specific features. For general information about any of the Communicator applications, it's best to begin with the Help Contents command.

To access online Help:

| STEP 3 | CLICK | Help Contents |

The NetHelp-Netscape window opens and contains the Overview page.

| STEP 4 | MAXIMIZE | the NetHelp-Netscape window, if necessary |

Your screen should look similar to Figure A-2.

FIGURE A-2

[Screenshot: NetHelp - Netscape window showing NETSCAPE COMMUNICATOR Overview page]

Left panel labels (with callout numbers):
- Contents, Index, Find (2)
- Communicator Overview
- **Overview**
- About Navigator
- About Messenger
- About Collabra
- About Composer
- About Conference
- About Netcaster
- About Calendar
- About IBM Host On-Demand
- About AutoAdmin
- Security
- User Profiles
- Error Messages
- Using Help (3)

Main panel:

Overview (1)

These are the main parts of Netscape Communicator; for more detailed information click any of these:

- Browsing the Web
- Sending and receiving email
- Using discussion groups (newsgroups) (1)
- Composing and editing Web pages
- Conferencing and group work tools

Buttons at bottom: (4) (5) (6) (7)

Taskbar: Start | Phoenix | Welcome to Netscape - ... | NetHelp - Netscape | 1:41 PM

Callout list (right margin):
1. Links to individual application online Help
2. Table of Contents, Index, and Find links
3. Table of Contents links
4. Back button
5. Forward button
6. Print button
7. Exit button

The Communicator Overview page contains two sets of links to each of the Communicator applications' online Help. You can open the online Help for an individual application by clicking one of the icon links at the top of the page or one of the text or icon links in the middle of the page. In the frame at the left of the page is a Table of Contents that contains links to online Help topics. Above the table of contents are three links that allow you to show the online Help Index, the online Help Table of Contents, and a Find dialog box you can use to search online Help by keyword. To review the links at the top of the page:

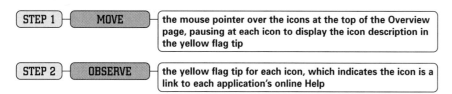

STEP 1 — MOVE — the mouse pointer over the icons at the top of the Overview page, pausing at each icon to display the icon description in the yellow flag tip

STEP 2 — OBSERVE — the yellow flag tip for each icon, which indicates the icon is a link to each application's online Help

Notice the links in the center of the page to the online Help for browsing the Web (Navigator), sending and receiving e-mail (Messenger), using newsgroups (Collabra), and creating Web pages (Composer).

To link to online Help for the Navigator browser:

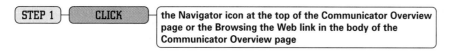

STEP 1 — CLICK — the Navigator icon at the top of the Communicator Overview page or the Browsing the Web link in the body of the Communicator Overview page

The Netscape Navigator online Help page loads. Your screen should look similar to Figure A-3.

FIGURE A-3

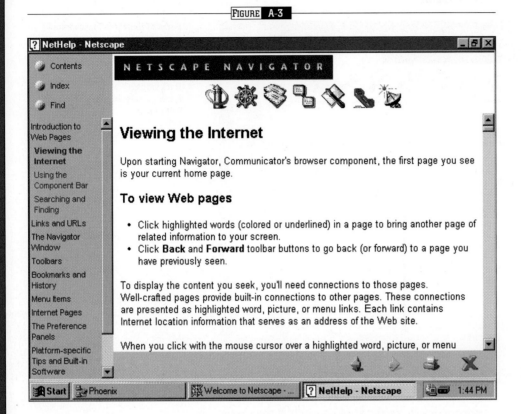

Each online Help window contains a Table of Contents for the current online Help page in a frame down the left side of the window. To observe the Table of Contents for the Netscape Navigator page:

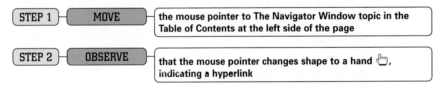

STEP 1   MOVE   the mouse pointer to The Navigator Window topic in the Table of Contents at the left side of the page

STEP 2   OBSERVE   that the mouse pointer changes shape to a hand 🖑, indicating a hyperlink

Your screen should look similar to Figure A-4.

FIGURE   A-4

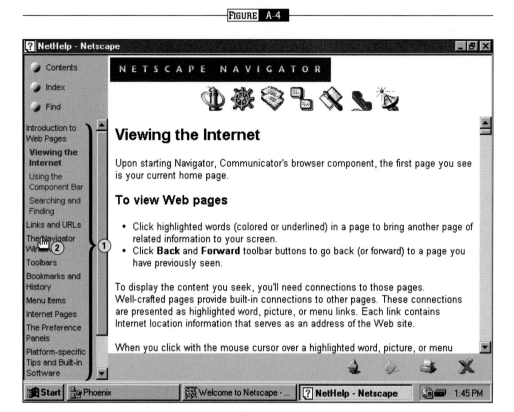

1. Table of Contents for Netscape Navigator Online Help
2. Mouse pointer on Table of Contents link

STEP 3 — OBSERVE — the remaining Table of Contents links

The NetHelp-Netscape window also contains shortcuts you can use to show the online index, to show the Table of Contents for the current online Help page, and to find specific words in the online Help page. Suppose you want to look up a specific word in online Help. You can use the index to do that.

To show the online Help index:

STEP 1 — CLICK — the Index button link in the top left corner of the NetHelp-Netscape window

In a few seconds, the online Help index appears in the frame, replacing the Table of Contents. Your screen should look similar to Figure A-5.

FIGURE A-5

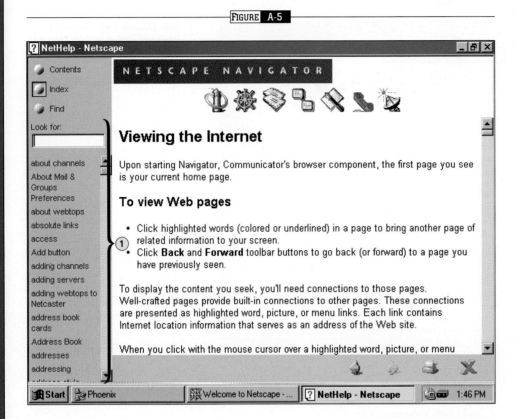

1. Online Help Index

Each word or phrase in the index is a link to the location in online Help where the word or phrase is discussed. You can scroll the index and click an item to review the online Help associated with it.

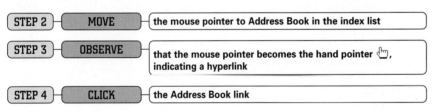

STEP 2 — MOVE — the mouse pointer to Address Book in the index list

STEP 3 — OBSERVE — that the mouse pointer becomes the hand pointer 👆, indicating a hyperlink

STEP 4 — CLICK — the Address Book link

A Help page with links to various Address Book topics loads. Your screen should look similar to Figure A-6.

FIGURE A-6

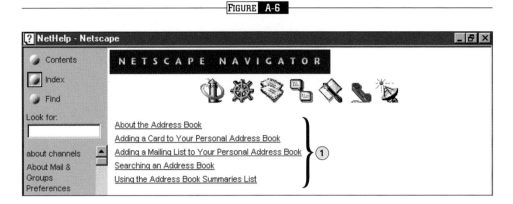

1. Links to Address Book topics

You also can search the index by typing a word or phrase in the Look for: text box, above the index list. When you type characters in the Look for: text box, a list of possible links appears in the index frame. For example, suppose you want to look for additional information about the Personal toolbar. You can scroll the index list to find Toolbars, or you can type the word "personal" in the Look for: text box, and the index will scroll to the section containing the word "personal." To search the index list for links to the Personal toolbar topic:

QUICK TIP

The index list scrolls up or down based on the characters you add or remove in the Look for: text box.

| STEP 1 | CLICK | inside the Look for: text box to position the insertion point, if necessary |

| STEP 2 | TYPE | personal |

As soon as you start typing the text "personal," the index list begins to scroll and a list of topics related to the text "personal" appears. The second topic is "personal toolbar." Your screen should look similar to Figure A-7.

FIGURE A-7

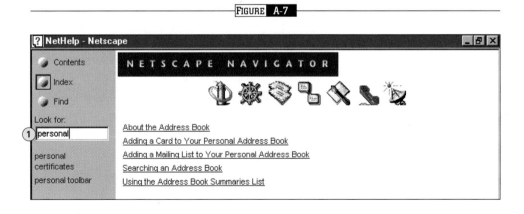

1. Search text typed in text box

STEP 3 — CLICK — the personal toolbar link in the index list

An online Help page with a link to <u>Using the Personal Toolbar</u> loads.

STEP 4 — CLICK — the **Using the Personal Toolbar link**

Individual topics in online Help are really part of one long online Help page. The portion of the online Help page that discusses the Personal toolbar now appears.

STEP 5 — SCROLL — the page and review the online Help text for using the personal toolbar

After you have finished using the index list, you can show the Table of Contents again by clicking the Contents button link in the top-left corner of the NetHelp-Netscape window. To view the Table of Contents:

STEP 1 — CLICK — the Contents link in the top-left corner of the NetHelp-Netscape window

The Table of Contents for the Toolbars topic appears in the frame. Remember that the Table of Contents items refer to the portion of the online Help page you currently are viewing. To view the top of the Table of Contents, you must return to the top of the Navigator online Help page. One way to view different sections of the online Help page is to use the Back and Forward navigation buttons in the bottom-right corner of the NetHelp-Netscape window.

To view the top of the Navigator online Help page:

STEP 1 — CLICK — the Back icon in the bottom-right corner of the NetHelp-Netscape window

The top of the Navigator online Help page appears in the NetHelp-Netscape window, and the Table of Contents automatically scrolls to the top of the Contents list.

You close the NetHelp-Netscape window by clicking the Close button on the title bar or the Exit icon in the bottom-right corner of the window.

To close the NetHelp-Netscape window:

STEP 1 — CLICK — the Close button on the title bar

QUICK TIP

You can print the online Help pages by clicking the Print icon in the bottom-right corner of the NetHelp-Netscape window.

A.b Loading Communicator Software Updates with SmartUpdate

When you purchase Communicator, you become a registered user. As a registered user, you can use the SmartUpdate feature to download Communicator updates and components directly from a file server to your computer. To update and install the correct release or add a missing component, Communicator uses the SmartUpdate feature to analyze your system to identify your operating system, software version, and language.

> **IN THIS APPENDIX**
>
> The steps in this appendix assume you are using the most current version of Communicator. If you are using an earlier version, different SmartUpdate Web pages with links for downloading the most current version of Communicator may appear. Follow any additional directions provided by your instructor.

Suppose you want to review the SmartUpdate Web pages to become familiar with the SmartUpdate process. *You will not actually download or install any software.* To review the SmartUpdate process:

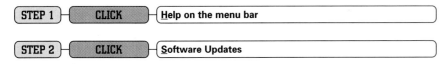

| STEP 1 | CLICK | **Help** on the menu bar |

| STEP 2 | CLICK | **Software Updates** |

The Communicator Rebate-Netscape Web page loads. Your screen should look similar to Figure A-8.

FIGURE A-8

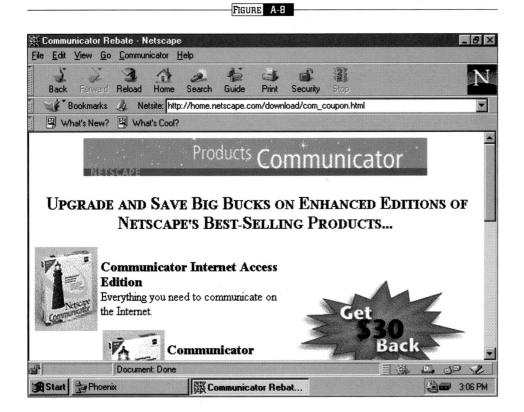

| STEP 1 | SCROLL | the page to locate the SmartUpdate link |

| STEP 2 | CLICK | the SmartUpdate link |

The second SmartUpdate-Netscape Web page loads. Your screen should look similar to Figure A-9.

FIGURE A-9

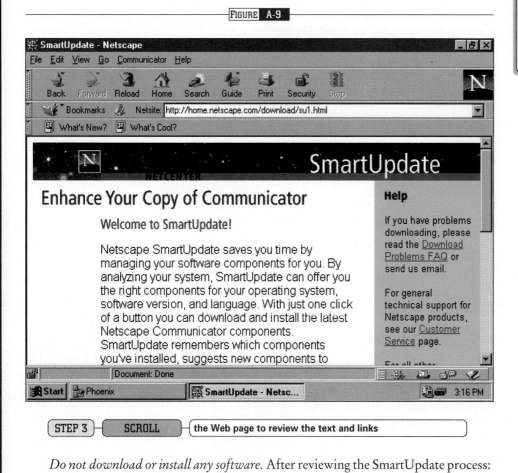

| STEP 3 | SCROLL | the Web page to review the text and links |

Do not download or install any software. After reviewing the SmartUpdate process:

| STEP 4 | RELOAD | the default home page |

Getting Information Automatically with Netscape Netcaster

Appendix Overview

Netscape Netcaster automatically delivers information from the Web to your desktop. That is made possible by a new kind of technology, which you will learn about in this appendix. You also will learn how to set up and use Netcaster to have the latest information on a variety of topics delivered to your computer.

S N A P S H O T

In this appendix you will learn to:

> **Describe push and pull technologies**

> **Start Netcaster**

> **Preview channels**

> **Subscribe to channels**

> **Delete channels**

B.a Describing Push and Pull Technologies

When you use Navigator to load a Web page, Navigator sends a request for the page to the Web server where the page is stored. That is called **pulling** the Web page to your computer. Netcaster uses a new form of Web technology, called **push** technology, to automatically deliver Web page content to your computer. All you have to do is specify what information you want and how often you want to receive it. To specify what information you want to receive, you must subscribe to a channel. A **channel** is a special type of Web site that uses push technology to broadcast Web page content to subscribers. For example, some news organizations like ABC News, CBS Sports, and CNNfn maintain Web channels to push, or broadcast, late-breaking news to their channel subscribers. The subscribed channel information is stored in cache like other Web pages, so you can browse the channel offline, if you want.

A **Webtop** is a special kind of channel that pushes its contents into a window on your desktop computer. A Webtop window can cover all or part of the screen and is hidden behind other open windows until you want to view it. Any channel can be made into a Webtop either when you subscribe to it or later, by revising the channel properties. You can use Netcaster channels and Webtops to automatically receive up-to-date information at your computer. For information about Webtops, click the Webtops Table of Contents link in Netcaster online Help.

IN THIS APPENDIX

In this appendix it is assumed that you have an ISP connection and that the Netcaster application is installed. If you do not have an ISP connection, or if the Netcaster application is not installed, you will not be able to do the hands-on activities.

B.b Starting Netcaster

After you start Netcaster, you can use the Channel Finder feature to preview and subscribe to channels or view a list of already subscribed-to channels. To start Netcaster:

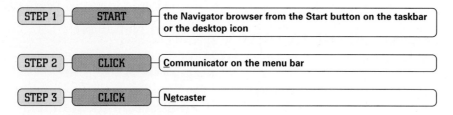

STEP 1	START	the Navigator browser from the Start button on the taskbar or the desktop icon
STEP 2	CLICK	Communicator on the menu bar
STEP 3	CLICK	Netcaster

The Starting Netcaster window appears in the middle of your screen, and Netcaster begins to load. After Netcaster is loaded, the Netcaster window appears by default on the right side of your screen. (If this is the first time you have used Netcaster, it may take several minutes to load.) By default, the Netscape Channel opens and appears in its own window. Because it constantly is being updated, the Netscape Channel you see on your screen will not be the same as the Netscape Channel in Figure B-1. However, your screen should look similar to Figure B-1.

FIGURE B-1

1. Netcaster window
2. Netscape Channel window
3. Netcaster window tab
4. Channel Finder and list of preselected channels
5. My Channels button
6. Command buttons
7. Webtop controls
8. Business Focus channel list tab
9. In General channel list tab

The Netcaster window overlaps any other maximized window on your screen (including the Netscape Channel window). To access all the features available in the Netscape Channel window, you first must temporarily hide the Netcaster window. You can hide or show the Netcaster window by clicking the Netcaster window tab. To hide the Netcaster window:

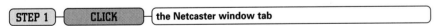

STEP 1 — CLICK — the Netcaster window tab

The Netcaster window is hidden temporarily, and only the Netcaster window tab is visible at the right side of your screen. When the Netcaster window is hidden, you can see all the features in the Netscape Channel window. The Netscape Channel automatically brings you up-to-date information about Netscape products and Internet issues.

To continue reviewing the Netcaster window, you need to "unhide" it. To unhide the Netcaster window:

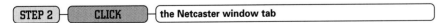

STEP 2 — CLICK — the Netcaster window tab

The Netcaster window again appears at the right side of your screen. The Netcaster window contains the Channel Finder button and a list of channels you can preview; the My Channels button, which is used to show a list of channels already subscribed to; a row of command buttons; and a row of Webtop controls.

QUICK TIP

You can change the default channel in Netcaster or specify that no channel open by clicking the Options button in the Netcaster window. In the Option dialog box click the Layout tab and select the desired default channel option.

The **Channel Finder** button allows you to preview preselected channels in two main categories: "Business Focus" and "In General." You also can view additional channels by clicking the "More Channels" button below the two category lists. To view the "Business Focus" channel list:

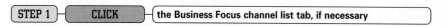
STEP 1 — CLICK — the Business Focus channel list tab, if necessary

The list of channels in the Business Focus group appears.

The **My Channels** button allows you to view a list of channels to which you already subscribe. To view the list of currently subscribed-to channels:

STEP 1 — CLICK — the My Channels button

The only channel currently subscribed to may be the Netscape Channel. When you install Netcaster, you are automatically subscribed to that channel. You will learn how to subscribe to, or add, other channels to the list in a later section.

To view the Business Focus channel list again:

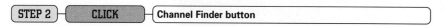
STEP 2 — CLICK — Channel Finder button

You use the **command buttons** below the My Channels button to add a channel to the My Channels list, set options for the Netcaster window, get online Help for Netcaster, and exit Netcaster.

You use the **Webtop controls** below the command buttons to show different Webtops, print a Webtop, alternately show a Webtop and the desktop, position a Webtop in front of or behind other open windows, and close a Webtop.

STEP 3 — USE — the mouse pointer and the yellow flag tip to review the command buttons and Webtop controls

Now that you are familiar with the components of the Netcaster window, you are ready to preview several channels and then subscribe to one.

B.c Previewing Channels

Suppose you want to preview the ABC News channel. To preview the channel, you simply click the desired channel button in the Channel Finder list. A small panel opens below the button showing you a mini-preview of the channel and providing two new buttons: one for viewing a larger preview in its own window and one for adding the channel to the My Channels list. To preview the ABCNEWS.com channel:

STEP 1 — CLICK — the ABCNEWS.com button

The mini-preview panel opens below the button.

To see a larger preview in its own window:

STEP 2 — CLICK — the Preview Channel button in the panel

The ABCNEWS.com channel opens in its own window, over the Netcaster window. It may take several minutes to finish loading the channel. After the channel is completely loaded your screen should look similar to Figure B-2.

FIGURE B-2

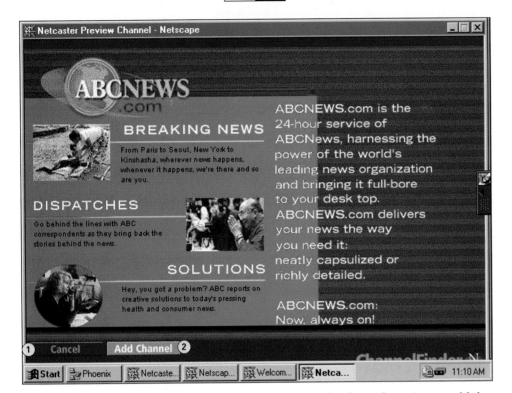

1. Cancel button
2. Add Channel button

After reviewing the larger preview, you can cancel the channel preview or add the channel to the My Channels list. To cancel the preview:

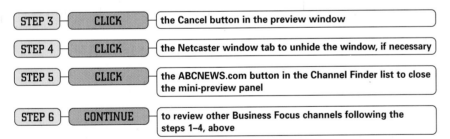

STEP 3	CLICK	the Cancel button in the preview window
STEP 4	CLICK	the Netcaster window tab to unhide the window, if necessary
STEP 5	CLICK	the ABCNEWS.com button in the Channel Finder list to close the mini-preview panel
STEP 6	CONTINUE	to review other Business Focus channels following the steps 1–4, above

After you finish previewing several channels, you are ready to subscribe to one.

B.d Subscribing to Channels

Suppose you decide to add the CNNfn channel to your My Channels list. To add the CNNfn channel to your list:

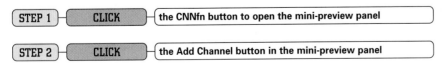

| STEP 1 | CLICK | the CNNfn button to open the mini-preview panel |
| STEP 2 | CLICK | the Add Channel button in the mini-preview panel |

In a few seconds the CNNfn Channel Setup window opens. You set your content preferences in this window. To accept the preset preferences and continue:

STEP 3 — CLICK — the Continue button at the bottom of the window

If you have not previously registered for free access to the Netcaster channels, the Netscape Adding a Channel window opens. If you are *not* a registered member:

STEP 4 — CLICK — the Continue button and then follow your instructor's directions for completing the membership and survey forms

If you *are* registered member, the CNNfn Setup page closes, the Netscape Channel page reappears, and the Channel Properties dialog box for the CNNfn channel opens.

STEP 1 — CLICK — the General tab, if necessary

You use the Channel Properties dialog box to specify how often you want the channel to be updated, how you want it to be displayed, and how many levels of information you want to store in cache for offline review.

The current setting specifies that the channel will update its information every 30 minutes. To change the setting to 2 hours:

STEP 1 — CLICK — the Update this channel list arrow

STEP 2 — CLICK — 2 HRS

The Display tab in the Channel Properties dialog box allows you to specify that the channel appear as a Webtop:

STEP 1 — CLICK — the Display tab in the Channel Properties dialog box

STEP 2 — OBSERVE — that the CNNfn channel will appear as a Webtop by default

Channels, like the Web pages you load in Navigator, are stored temporarily in hard-disk storage called cache. You can specify the amount of cache, or storage area, to allocate to the channel and how many levels of content (linked pages) you want to store. For example, you may want to store only the primary channel page and any second-level pages linked to the primary page. That would be two levels of content.

STEP 3 — CLICK — the Cache tab in the Channel Properties dialog box

STEP 4 — OBSERVE — that the two levels of content for the CNNfn channel will be stored in cache for offline browsing

STEP 5 — CLICK — OK to close the dialog box

The CNNfn channel is now added to the My Channels list. To review the My Channels list:

STEP 6 — UNHIDE — the Netscape window, if necessary

CAUTION

If a moving red progress line appears below the channel name, the channel is being updated. Because viewing a channel while it is being updated extends the update time, avoid viewing a channel until updating is complete. After the update process has finished, the moving red progress line is no longer visible.

The CNNfn Channel appears in the My Channels list. Note the small square icon at the far right of the channel name, indicates that the channel is a Webtop.

To view the revised My Channels list:

STEP 1	CLICK	the CNNfn button in the Channel Finder list to close the mini-preview panel
STEP 2	CLICK	the My Channels button
STEP 3	OBSERVE	that the CNNfn channel is added to the list

To view the contents of any channel, simply open the Netcaster window, click the My Channels button, and then click the desired channel in the list. Because the CNNfn channel was added as a Webtop, you also will use a Webtop control at the bottom of the Netcaster window to view it. To view the contents of the CNNfn channel:

| STEP 1 | CLICK | the CNNfn channel in the list |

While the CNNfn channel loads, the Netcaster window is hidden temporarily, and the Netscape Channel page appears. To view the CNNfn Webtop, you will use the Show or Hide Webtop control:

| STEP 2 | UNHIDE | the Netcaster window, if necessary |
| STEP 3 | CLICK | the Show or Hide Webtop control (the fifth control from the left) at the bottom of the Netcaster window |

The CNNfn Webtop appears.

| STEP 4 | HIDE | the Netcaster window, if necessary |

Notice that the CNNfn Webtop covers the entire screen. When you view a Webtop, the Netscape icon and Webtop controls remain visible in the lower-right part of your screen. After reviewing the CNNfn Webtop, you should close it. To close the Webtop:

| STEP 5 | CLICK | the Close the Webtop control (the seventh control from the left) in the lower-right corner of your screen |

Occasionally you may want to delete a channel from the My Channels list. In the next section you will delete the CNNfn channel from the My Channels list.

B.e Deleting Channels

When you are no longer interested in automatically receiving information from a channel, you can delete it. Suppose you no longer want to review the CNNfn channel. To delete the CNNfn channel:

| STEP 1 | CLICK | the Options button at the bottom of the Netcaster window |

QUICK TIP

You can add some channels directly by clicking a button on the channel page. If you are viewing a channel (Web site) in Navigator and a button is provided, click the button and follow the directions to add the channel to your My channels list.

The Options - Netscape dialog box opens.

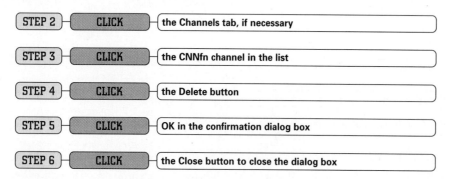

STEP 2 — CLICK — the Channels tab, if necessary

STEP 3 — CLICK — the CNNfn channel in the list

STEP 4 — CLICK — the Delete button

STEP 5 — CLICK — OK in the confirmation dialog box

STEP 6 — CLICK — the Close button to close the dialog box

The CNNfn channel is removed from the My Channels list. To show the Channel Finder list, close Netcaster and then close Navigator:

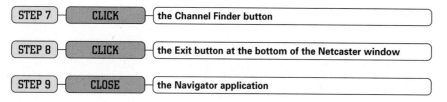

STEP 7 — CLICK — the Channel Finder button

STEP 8 — CLICK — the Exit button at the bottom of the Netcaster window

STEP 9 — CLOSE — the Navigator application

For more information on using Netcaster's layout options and Webtop controls, see online Help.

Participating in Newsgroups with Netscape Collabra

Appendix Overview

Newsgroups are Internet discussion groups in which participants with common interests (such as business, professional associations, or television shows) share information by posting articles or messages to the USENET network. Interested Internet users around the world can read the articles and respond to them by writing and posting their own articles, sending e-mail messages to the articles' authors, or both.

SNAPSHOT

In this appendix you will learn to:

> **View a list of news-groups**

> **Subscribe to a news-group**

> **Read and respond to newsgroup articles**

> **Unsubscribe to a newsgroup**

IN THIS APPENDIX

In this appendix it is assumed you have an ISP connection and at least one newsgroup server listed in the Message Center window. If you do not have an ISP connection or access to a newsgroup server, you can read the steps to view, subscribe, and unsubscribe to newsgroups.

C.a Viewing a List of Newsgroups

The Netscape Collabra application allows you to participate in newsgroups. In this appendix, you will learn how to subscribe to a newsgroup, read and respond to newsgroup articles, and unsubscribe to a newsgroup.

To start Netscape Collabra:

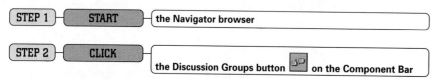

STEP 1 — START — the Navigator browser

STEP 2 — CLICK — the Discussion Groups button ◻ on the Component Bar

The Netscape Message Center window, the primary Collabra window, opens.

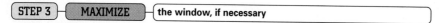

STEP 3 — MAXIMIZE — the window, if necessary

Your screen should look similar to Figure C-1.

FIGURE C-1

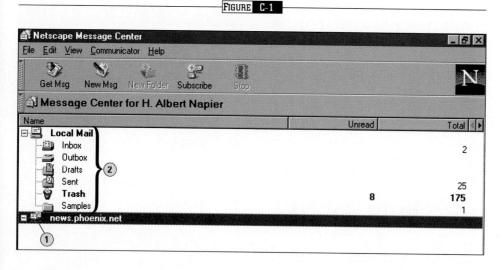

1. Newsgroup folder
2. Mail folders

The Message Center window contains your mail and newsgroup folders. There should be at least one newsgroup folder in the window. To see a list of the newsgroups provided by your ISP:

STEP 4 — CLICK — the Subscribe button ◻ on the Navigation toolbar

The Communicator: Subscribe to Discussion Groups dialog box opens, and in a few seconds a list of the available newsgroups appears in the All Groups tab.

The list of newsgroups is organized much like the list of files and folders you see in Windows Explorer. The list consists of individual newsgroups and folders that contain multiple newsgroups. When there are many newsgroups about the same general topic, they are organized in a folder for that topic. Individual newsgroups are represented by a set of small message-balloon icons. Folders that contain multiple newsgroups are represented by folder icons.

Newgroups are identified by name, which can consist of a general topic (like entertainment) and a subtopic (like movies). Some newsgroup names also may contain third and fourth topic levels. Each topic level serves to narrow the scope of the discussions within the newsgroup. The general topic level may be one of several commonly used topics, like "biz" for business topics or "alt" for alternative topics.

For example, the business, or "biz," category includes many business-related newsgroups. Suppose you are interested in exchanging information about computer hardware and software for business applications. You might find newsgroups named "biz.comp.hardware" and "biz.comp.software." The general topic is business (biz); the first subtopic is computers (comp), and the second subtopic is hardware or software. The participants in these newsgroups limit their discussions to computer hardware or software for business.

QUICK TIP

The first time you open the Subscribe to Discussion Groups dialog box, you will have to get a list of available groups from your ISP. To do that, click the Get Groups button. It will take several minutes for the list to be created the first time. Also, the first time you look at newsgroups, Collabra may open the Mail & Discussion Groups Wizard so you can set your newsgroup preferences.

IN THIS APPENDIX

If the newsgroups and folders used in the appendix examples are not available from your news server, you can substitute similar newsgroups and folders from your list.

You expand or collapse the newsgroup folders just as you expand or collapse folders in Windows Explorer. To expand and then collapse the academ.* folder:

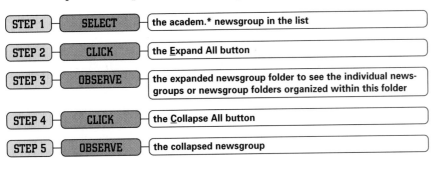

STEP 1	SELECT	the academ.* newsgroup in the list
STEP 2	CLICK	the Expand All button
STEP 3	OBSERVE	the expanded newsgroup folder to see the individual newsgroups or newsgroup folders organized within this folder
STEP 4	CLICK	the Collapse All button
STEP 5	OBSERVE	the collapsed newsgroup

To locate and expand the business-related newsgroups folder:

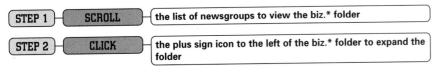

| STEP 1 | SCROLL | the list of newsgroups to view the biz.* folder |
| STEP 2 | CLICK | the plus sign icon to the left of the biz.* folder to expand the folder |

To collapse the biz.* folder:

| STEP 3 | CLICK | the minus sign to the left of the biz.* folder |

You can continue to scroll and review different newsgroups by name and then click the Subscribe button to add the newsgroup to your list of subscribed newsgroups. You also can search for specific newsgroups by a keyword that appears in the newsgroup name. For example, suppose you want to find newsgroups related to finding business jobs. You might begin by searching for "biz.jobs" to find newsgroups related to jobs in the business area. An alternative might be to search for "jobs" to get a list of all job-related newsgroups, not just those in the business area. To search for specific newsgroups:

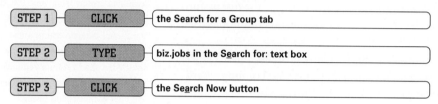

STEP 1 — CLICK — the Search for a Group tab

STEP 2 — TYPE — biz.jobs in the Search for: text box

STEP 3 — CLICK — the Search Now button

In a few seconds the newsgroups that contain the keywords "biz.jobs" in their name appear in the Discussion group name list. If you do not get results using "biz.jobs," try searching for "jobs."

After you find a newsgroup that interests you, the next step is to subscribe to the group so you can read and respond to articles posted to the group. In the next section you will subscribe to one of the newsgroups you just found.

C.b Subscribing to a Newsgroup

Subscribing to a newsgroup means adding the newsgroup to a short list that appears in the Message Center window when you expand the news server folder. After you subscribe to a newsgroup, you can read and respond to articles posted to the group. To subscribe to a newsgroup:

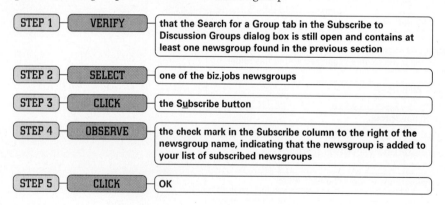

STEP 1 — VERIFY — that the Search for a Group tab in the Subscribe to Discussion Groups dialog box is still open and contains at least one newsgroup found in the previous section

STEP 2 — SELECT — one of the biz.jobs newsgroups

STEP 3 — CLICK — the Subscribe button

STEP 4 — OBSERVE — the check mark in the Subscribe column to the right of the newsgroup name, indicating that the newsgroup is added to your list of subscribed newsgroups

STEP 5 — CLICK — OK

The dialog box closes, and you return to the Message Center window. To view the subscribed-to newsgroups, you must expand the news server folder (if it is not already expanded). If a plus sign appears to the left of the news server folder, the folder is not expanded. To expand the news server folder, if necessary:

| STEP 1 | OBSERVE | a plus sign to the left of the news server folder, indicating that the news server folder can be expanded |
| STEP 2 | CLICK | the plus sign |

The subscribed-to newsgroups appear below the expanded news server folder. You also will see the total number of articles (messages) in the group, and the number of unread articles. Each time you open the Message Center window, the subscribed-to newsgroups are updated with new articles. Your screen should look similar to Figure C-2.

FIGURE C-2

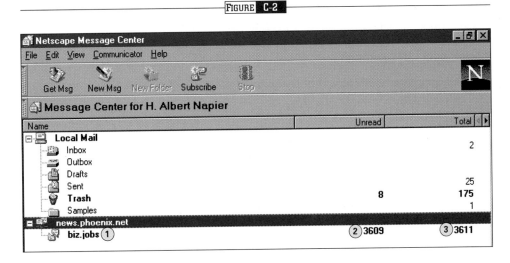

1. Subscribed-to newsgroups
2. Total number of unread messages in the group
3. Total number of messages in the group

Whenever you want, you can open the Message Center window and read the articles posted to the group. In the next section you will learn how to read a newsgroup article.

C.c Reading and Responding to Newsgroup Articles

Reading a newsgroup article is like reading incoming e-mail. When you select a newsgroup to browse new articles, the articles open in the Message List window. The Message List window looks like the Inbox window, and you follow the same steps to read and reply to a newsgroup article as you would an e-mail message. (For more information on using e-mail, see Chapter 3.)

MENU TIP

You get new discussion group messages by pointing to the Get Messages command on the File menu and then clicking the New command.

To read an article from the biz.jobs newsgroup:

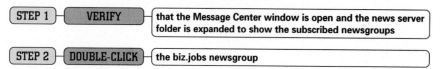

STEP 1 — **VERIFY** — that the Message Center window is open and the news server folder is expanded to show the subscribed newsgroups

STEP 2 — **DOUBLE-CLICK** — the biz.jobs newsgroup

MOUSE TIP

You get new discussion group messages by clicking the Get Messages button on the Navigation toolbar.

If this is the first time you are reading articles in this newsgroup, the Download Headers dialog box may open, indicating the number of unread message headers in the group. In this dialog box you can choose to download all the unread message headers or specify the number of message headers you want to download. If the Download Headers dialog box opens, complete steps 3–5:

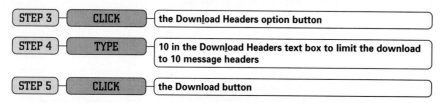

STEP 3 — **CLICK** — the Download Headers option button

STEP 4 — **TYPE** — 10 in the Download Headers text box to limit the download to 10 message headers

STEP 5 — **CLICK** — the Download button

The Message List window opens and displays a list of article or message headers. To read a specific article, simply click the article header and read the contents of the article in the Message pane. The list of article headers you see will likely be different from the list shown in Figure E-6.

To read an article:

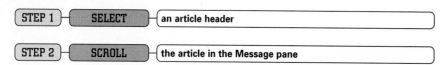

STEP 1 — **SELECT** — an article header

STEP 2 — **SCROLL** — the article in the Message pane

A response to a newsgroup article is called a **thread**. You can respond by posting a thread to the group only or by posting a thread to both the group and the author of the original article. To do that, simply select the article header, click the Reply button on the Navigation toolbar, then click either Reply to Group or Reply to Sender and Group. The Message Composition window will open, and you can type and send your response. *Do not respond to an article at this time.* To close the Message List window:

STEP 3 — **CLICK** — the Close button ☒ on the Message List window title bar

If you are no longer interested in a specific newsgroup, you can "unsubscribe" to it. Doing so removes the newsgroup from the short list in the Message Center window but does not remove it from the newsgroup list maintained by your ISP. You can resubscribe later, if you want. In the next section you will unsubscribe to the biz.jobs newsgroup.

C.d Unsubscribing to a Newsgroup

The process of **unsubscribing** to a newsgroup is similar to the process of subscribing to a newsgroup. First, you must open the Subscribe to Discussion Groups dialog box, select the newsgroup (either from the complete list or by searching for the newsgroup by keyword), and then remove the check mark by clicking the Unsubscribe button. To unsubscribe to the biz.jobs newsgroup:

| STEP 1 | VERIFY | that the Message Center window is open |

| STEP 2 | CLICK | the Subscribe button 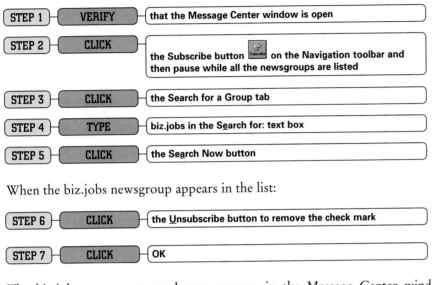 on the Navigation toolbar and then pause while all the newsgroups are listed |

| STEP 3 | CLICK | the Search for a Group tab |

| STEP 4 | TYPE | biz.jobs in the Search for: text box |

| STEP 5 | CLICK | the Search Now button |

When the biz.jobs newsgroup appears in the list:

| STEP 6 | CLICK | the Unsubscribe button to remove the check mark |

| STEP 7 | CLICK | OK |

The biz.jobs newsgroup no longer appears in the Message Center window.

| STEP 1 | CLOSE | the Message Center window |

| STEP 2 | CLOSE | Navigator |

For more information on using Collabra to participate in newsgroups, see online Help. Another good source of information on newsgroups is the Web. There are many Web sites devoted to information about newsgroups. Try searching with the keyword "newsgroups" or "newsgroups FAQ" to find Web sites with newsgroup information or answers to frequently asked questions (FAQ) about newsgroups.

Many newsgroup lists also include several newsgroups under the main topic "news." Such newsgroups are devoted to discussing how to participate in newsgroups. You can find good information, like how to request a new newsgroup be created or newsgroup etiquette (part of the Netiquette discussed in Chapter 3).

Tips for Finding Information on the Web

D.a — Tips for Searching the Web

Before you begin looking for information on the Web, it is a good idea to think about what you want to accomplish, establish a time frame in which to find the information, and then develop a search strategy. As you search, keep in mind the following guidelines:

- To find broad, general information, start with a Web directory like Galaxy or Yahoo.
- To find a specific Web page, start with a search engine like Alta Vista or HotBot.
- Take time to become familiar with a variety of different search engines and their features. Remember that many search engines are revised frequently. It is important to look for revisions to the search engines you use on a regular basis.
- Search engines use robot programs to index all the pages on the Web. However, because search engine robot programs work independently of each other, not all search engines have the same index of Web pages at any one time. Be prepared to use multiple search engines for each search.
- Always take time to review a search engine's online Help the first time you use that search engine.
- Boolean operators allow you to combine or exclude keywords when using a search engine. Proximal operators allow you specify that search keywords be close together in a Web page. Remember, not all search engines support Boolean and Proximal operators. However, to reduce the scope of your search, use the AND (+), OR, and NOT (-) Boolean operators and the NEAR and FOLLOWED BY Proximal operators whenever possible. For example, when searching for Web pages containing international business accounting information, try searching by the keywords *"international business"* **and** *accounting*. If you are looking for gold or silver, try searching by the keywords *metals* **not** *heavy,* so you don't get pages devoted to heavy-metal rock music. To make sure the keywords are in close proximity to each other, use the proximal operators NEAR and FOLLOWED BY.
- Be specific with the keywords or phrases you use. The more specific the phrase, the more efficient your search will be. For example, use the phrase international business plus the word accounting (*"international business"* **+** *accounting*) rather than simply *accounting* if you want to find Web pages that contain international business accounting information.
- Watch your spelling. Be aware how the search engine you use handles capitalization. In one search engine, "pear" may match "Pear," "pEaR," or "PEAR." In another search engine, "Pear" may match only "Pear."
- Think of related words and phrases that might return the information you need. For example, if you were searching for information about oil, you might use "petroleum" and "petrochemicals," in addition to "oil."

- Search for common variations of word usage or spelling. For example, searching on the keywords "deep sea drilling," "deepsea drilling," and "deep-sea drilling" all may provide useful information.
- The search returns (or hits) usually are listed in order of relevance. You may find that only the first 10 or 12 hits are useful. To find more relevant Web pages, try searching again with different keywords.
- After you find the desired information, remember that the Web is largely unregulated and that anyone can put anything on a Web page. You need to evaluate carefully the credibility of all the information you find. Try to find out something about the author and his or her credentials or about the validity of the source. It is a good idea to find supporting information from another source before you use Web-based information for critical business decisions. A good place to look for guidelines to locating and evaluating Web-based information is college and university online library Web pages.

Index

U

Uniform Resource Locators (URLs), 10, 56
finding, to load Web pages, 75-77
Unsubscribing to newsgroup, AP-25
Uploading, 5, 6, 166
USENET network, 10, 22, AP-19
User name, 10

V

Vendor information, getting, 124-126
Viruses, computer, 46

W

Weather reports, getting, 109-110
Web browser(s), 6, 7
Navigator, 5, 7
WebCrawler, 61, 85
Web page(s), 6, 19, 56
designing effective, 141-142
loading, 75-77
printing, 65-66
publishing, 166-169
pulling and pushing, AP-12
reloading, 80
saving, 65
secure/insecure, 87-88
stored at your computer, viewing, 149-152

testing, 165-166
using Composer to create, 152-164
using HTML to create, 142-152
viewing HTML source for, 143
Web servers, 55
Web site(s), 6, 56, 86
defining structure of, 140-141
promoting, 169
setting goals and objectives for, 140
Webtop, AP-12
Webtop controls, AP-14
What's Cool? button, 82
What's New? button, 82
Width=100%, 146
Windows 95, 5
WORLDCC.GIF image file, 148, 149, 157, 163
WORLD.HTML Web page, 149-152
WORLDWIDE.HTML file, 160, 167
World Wide Web (WWW), 6, 11, 55
connecting to, 7
finding entertainment activities and restaurants on, 107-109
identifying common business tasks on, 96-97

locating city maps on, 105-107
locating travel-related information on, 96-97, 109-110
making hotel reservations and renting car on, 101-105
making travel arrangements on, 96-97
researching flight schedules on, 97-101
searching, with Navigator search page, 85-86
tips for searching, AP-27–AP-28
understanding, 56

X

Xeon Data Systems, 10, 34

Y

Yahoo!, 60, 86
Yellow Pages command, 87